easy crochet
Seaside

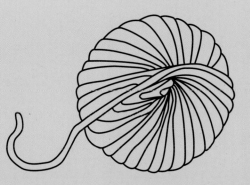

easy crochet
Seaside

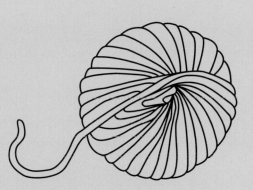

30 projects to make for your home and to wear

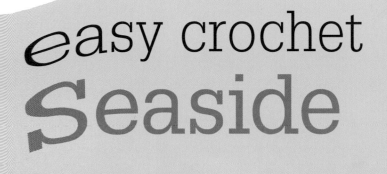

Consultant: Nikki Trench

hamlyn

An Hachette UK Company
www.hachette.co.uk

First published in Great Britain in 2013 by
Hamlyn, a division of Octopus Publishing Group Ltd
Endeavour House
189 Shaftesbury Avenue
London
WC2H 8JY
www.octopusbooks.co.uk

ISBN 978-0-600-62835-4

A CIP catalogue record for this book is available from the
British Library

Printed and bound in China

10 9 8 7 6 5 4 3 2 1

easy crochet
Seaside

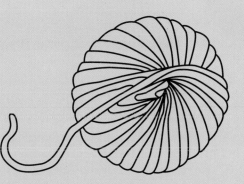

30 projects to make for your home and to wear

Consultant: Nikki Trench

hamlyn

An Hachette UK Company
www.hachette.co.uk

First published in Great Britain in 2013 by
Hamlyn, a division of Octopus Publishing Group Ltd
Endeavour House
189 Shaftesbury Avenue
London
WC2H 8JY
www.octopusbooks.co.uk

ISBN 978-0-600-62835-4

A CIP catalogue record for this book is available from the
British Library

Printed and bound in China

10 9 8 7 6 5 4 3 2 1

Contents

Introduction 6

Supersize bag 8

Textured boxy cardigan 12

Handbag doorstop 16

Mesh-pattern top 20

Funky throw 24

Striped beach bag 28

Bold striped cardigan 32

Seaside cushion 36

Beach duffle bag 40

Sun hat with floppy brim 44

Zingy round cushion 48

Cobweb wrap 52

Bead-trimmed beach bag 56

Waterfall jacket 60

Work-of-art scarf 64

Nautical sweater 68

Colour-block throw 72

Stetson-style hat 76

Poncho coat 80

Mini rag-rug placemats 84

Loop-neck sweater 88

Fish bath mat 92

Colour-block sweater 96

Lace towel edging 100

Gingham shopping bag 104

Striped beach poncho 108

Shades of orange rug 112

Beaded curtain 116

Round and square cushion pair 120

Summer tote bag 124

Index 128

Introduction

Crochet is easy, and it grows fast. Master a few basic stitches (and the terminology) and you can create stylish crocheted items to wear, use to decorate your home and as gifts for friends and family in next to no time and with minimal experience.

Whether you are a relative beginner, a confident convert or a long-term aficionado, there are projects here to delight. While your first attempts may be a bit uneven, a little practice and experimentation will ensure you soon improve. None of the projects in this book is beyond the scope of even those fairly new to the hobby. Even the most basic of stitches can be translated into covetable items.

Who doesn't love to be beside the seaside? All the projects in this book conjure wide horizons and sun, sea and sand. Make a tote or duffle bag for your beach essentials, crochet yourself a hat and get out there. Sea breezes can be brisk, however, so there are scarves, cardigans or a poncho to make. If you are staying at home, there are tempting nautical projects for you to enjoy there, too, such as place mats and a bath mat.

Crochet essentials

All you really need to get crocheting is a hook and some yarn. For many projects that's it, and where additional items are required, most of these can be found in a fairly basic sewing kit. All measurements are given in metric and imperial. Choose which to work in and stick with it since conversions may not be exact in all instances.

- **Hooks** These are sized in mm (with 'old UK' sizes given as well) and can be made from wood, plastic, aluminium, bamboo or steel. The material affects the weight and 'feel' of the hook, and which you choose is largely down to personal preference.
- **Yarns** Specific yarns are given for each project, but if you want to make substitutions, full details of the yarn's composition and the ball lengths are given so that you can choose alternatives, either from the wide range of online sources, or from your local supplier,

many of whom have very knowledgeable staff. Do keep any leftover yarns (not forgetting the ball bands, since these contain vital information) to use for future projects.
- **Additional items** Some of the projects require making up and finishing, and need further materials and equipment, such as needles (both ordinary and round-pointed tapestry ones) and thread, buttons, ribbons and other accessories. These are detailed for each project in the Getting Started box.

What is in this book

All projects are illustrated with several photographs to show you the detail of the work – both inspirational and useful for reference. A full summary of each project is given in the Getting Started box so you can see exactly what's involved. Here, projects are graded from one star (straightforward, suitable for beginners) through two (more challenging) to three stars (for crocheters with more confidence and experience).

Also in the Getting Started box is the size of each finished item, yarn(s) and additional materials needed, and what tension the project is worked in. Finally, a breakdown of the steps involved is given so you know exactly what the project entails before you start.

At the start of the pattern instructions is a key to all abbreviations particular to the project and occasional notes expand if necessary.

Additional information

Occasionally, more information or a specialist technique is needed. How To boxes and diagrams clarify these potentially tricky steps. The box on page 87, for example, explains how to cut the fabric for the rag-rug mats, while on page 27 a diagram shows where to position the shaped motifs on the throw.

If you have enjoyed the projects here, you may want to explore the other titles in the Easy Crochet series: *Babies & Children*, *Country*, *Flowers*, *Vintage & Retro* and *Weekend*. For those who enjoy knitting, a sister series Easy Knitting, features similarly stylish yet simple projects.

Supersize bag

Strong and practical, this over-sized bag can carry all your shopping or everything for a day on the beach.

From a base of plain craft cotton combined with leftover balls of colourful DK to give a variegated striped effect, this double crochet bag is lined with a striking bold print to give a strong and stable hold-all.

GETTING STARTED

★ ★ *Easy stitch and construction but working with three yarns and sewing a fabric lining all require care.*

Size:
51cm (20in) wide x 38cm (15in) deep

How much yarn:
3 x 100g (3½oz) balls of King Cole Craft Cotton in each of two colours – Natural (shade 46) and Whitewash (shade 301)
Leftover DK yarn in colourful shades of pink, turquoise and green

Hook:
10mm (UK 000) crochet hook

Additional items:
130 x 49cm (51 x 19in) rectangle of patterned cotton fabric
Sewing needle and matching thread

Tension:
10 sts and 12 rows measure 10cm (4in) square over dc using three strands of yarn on 10mm (UK 000) hook
IT IS ESSENTIAL TO WORK TO THE STATED TENSION TO ACHIEVE SUCCESS

What you have to do:
Work with three strands of yarn throughout – see Notes. Work bag base in rows of double crochet and then work sides in continuous rounds. Sew fabric lining and handles for bag. Stitch lining into bag.

The Yarn
King Cole Craft Cotton (approx. 133m/ 145 yards per 100g/3½oz ball) contains 90% cotton and 10% other fibres. It is available in cream and white only; here it is combined with DK yarn.

Instructions

Abbreviations:

ch = chain(s)
cm = centimetre(s)
cont = continue
dc = double crochet
patt = pattern
rep = repeat
RS = right side
ss = slip stitch
st(s) = stitch(es)
WS = wrong side

Notes:

Bag is worked with three strands of yarn throughout. For the lighter rounds, use both cream and white craft cotton along with one strand of coloured DK yarn, and for the darker rounds, use one strand of craft cotton with two strands of coloured DK yarn. Change the yarns every three or four rounds to form stripes.

BAG:
Base:

With 10mm (UK 000) hook and three strands of yarn, make 39ch.

Foundation row: 1dc into 2nd ch from hook, 1dc into each ch to end, turn.

1st–9th rows: 1ch (counts as first dc), miss dc at base of ch, 1dc into each dc, 1dc in 1ch, turn. 39dc.

Sides:

1st round: 1ch, miss dc at base of ch, 1dc into each dc, 1dc in 1ch, do not turn but cont to work around outer edges of base, *2dc into first row end,

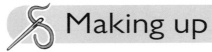

1dc into each of next 8 row ends, 2dc into last row end *, 1dc into base of each foundation ch, rep from * to * once more, join with a ss into first ch. 102 sts.
Work in continuous rounds of dc until bag sides are 30cm (12in) high. Work another 10 rounds in dc (as these final rounds will be covered by fabric, you can use up ends of yarn in leftover colours). Fasten off.

Making up

Lining:

Cut a 104 x 49cm (41 x 19in) rectangle of patterned fabric. Fold in half widthways with RS facing and, taking 1cm (⅜in) seam allowances, join side and lower edges. Press under a 1cm (⅜in) hem to WS around top edge, then press under a further 10cm (4in) deep turning. Slip lining inside bag, matching seam to side of bag. Fold turning back over final 10 rounds at top edge of bag and pin in place. Sew around folded edge of lining, taking needle right through to inside with each stitch to hold securely in place.

Handles:

From the remaining fabric cut two strips, each 13 x 43cm (5 x 17in) of patterned fabric. Press each strip in half lengthways, with WS facing. Open out fold, then turn in raw edges so that they lie along centre crease. Press new folds. Turn up 1cm (⅜in) at each end, then press handles in half lengthwise. Top-stitch around all sides, 3mm (⅛in) in from edges.

Pin handles to inside, 18cm (7in) in from side edges of bag, with an overlap of 3cm (1¼in). Stab stitch very securely in place through bag and lining, using a double length of sewing thread for strength.

Textured boxy cardigan

A classic shape is given an interesting twist with this beautiful textured yarn.

A chunky yarn with silky slubs creates a beautiful textured fabric for this classic cardigan with distinctive buttons.

GETTING STARTED

 Simple stitch pattern, but plenty of shaping and fabric should be neat for a good result.

Size:

To fit bust: 82–86[92–97:102–107]cm (32–34[36–38:40–42]in)

Actual size: 96[107:116]cm (37¾[42:45¼]in)

Length: 54[56:57.5]cm (21¼[22:22¾]in)

Sleeve seam: 46cm (18in)

Note: Figures in square brackets [ ] refer to larger sizes; where there is only one set of figures, it applies to all sizes

How much yarn:

13[14:14] x 50g (1¾oz) balls of Louisa Harding Rossetti in turquoise (shade 4)

Hooks:

7.00mm (UK 2) crochet hook

8.00mm (UK 0) crochet hook

Additional items:

6 buttons

Tension:

10 sts and 12 rows measure 10cm (4in) square over dc on 8.00mm (UK 0) hook

IT IS ESSENTIAL TO WORK TO THE STATED TENSION TO ACHIEVE SUCCESS

What you have to do:

Work throughout in double crochet. Use simple shaping for armholes, neck and sleeve shaping. Make buttonholes as directed in right front edge. Work crab stitch edging (double crochet worked from left to right) around outer edges.

The Yarn

Louisa Harding Rossetti (approx. 70m/76 yards per 50g/1¾oz ball) contains 67% merino wool, 28% silk and 5% polyamide. This chunky yarn is hand wash only. It has silky slubs, which creates an interesting, glistening fabric. There is a small palette of strong colours.

Instructions

BACK:

With 8.00mm (UK 0) hook make 49[54:59]ch.

Foundation row: (RS) 1dc into 2nd ch from hook, 1dc into each ch to end, turn.

Patt row: 1ch (counts as first dc), miss st at base of ch, 1dc into each dc to end, turn. 48[53:58] sts. Cont in patt, rep last row 38 times more. Fasten off.

Shape armholes:

Next row: (RS) Miss 2[2:3] sts, rejoin yarn to next st, 1ch, 1dc into each of next 43[48:51] sts, turn. 44[49:52] sts.

Abbreviations:

alt = alternate

ch = chain(s)

cm = centimetre(s)

cont = continue

dc = double crochet

dc2tog = into each of next 2 sts work: (insert hook into st, yrh and draw through a loop), yrh and draw through all 3 loops on hook

dec = decrease(d)

foll = following

inc = increase(d)

patt = pattern

rem = remain(ing)

rep = repeat

RS = right side

ss = slip stitch

st(s) = stitch(es)

tog = together

tr = treble

WS = wrong side

yrh = yarn round hook

Next row: 1ch, miss st at base of ch, dc2tog over next 2 sts, 1dc into each st to last 3 sts, dc2tog over next 2 sts, 1dc into last st, turn. 1 st dec at each end of row. Rep last row 4[5:5] times more. 34[37:40] sts. Work 16[17:19] rows straight.

Shape neck:

Next row: (RS) 1ch, miss st at base of ch, 1dc into each of next 6[7:8] sts, dc2tog over next 2 sts, 1tr into next st, turn.

Next row: 2ch, miss st at base of ch,

dc2tog over next 2 sts, 1dc into each st to end. 8[9:10] sts. Fasten off.

Next row: (RS) Miss centre 14[15:16] sts, rejoin yarn into next st, 2ch, dc2tog over next 2 sts, 1dc into each st to end, turn.

Next row: Patt to last 3 sts, dc2tog over next 2 sts, 1tr into 2nd of 2ch. 8[9:10] sts. Fasten off.

LEFT FRONT:

With 8.00mm (UK 0) hook make 27[30:32]ch. Work foundation row as given for Back. 26[29:31] sts. Cont in patt as given for Back until 40 rows in all have been completed. Fasten off.

Shape armhole:

Next row: (RS) Miss 2[2:3] sts, rejoin yarn to next st, 1ch, 1dc into each of rem 23[26:27] sts.

Dec one st as before at armhole edge on next 5[6:6] rows. 19[21:22] sts. Work 8[9:9] rows straight.

Shape neck:

1st row: (RS) Patt 9[10:11] sts, dc2tog over next 2 sts, 1tr into next st, turn.

2nd row: 2ch, miss st at base of ch, dc2tog over next 2 sts, 1dc into each st to end, turn.

3rd row: Patt to last 3 sts, dc2tog over next 2 sts, 1tr into last st, turn.

4th row: As 2nd row. 8[9:10] sts.
Work 6[6:8] rows straight. Fasten off.

RIGHT FRONT:

With 8.00mm (UK 0) hook make 27[30:32]ch. Work foundation row as given for Back. 26[29:31] sts. Cont in patt as given for Back until 12[14:14] rows in all have been completed.

1st buttonhole row: (RS) 1ch, miss st at base of ch, 1dc into next st, 2ch, miss next 2 sts, 1dc into each st to end, turn.
Working 1dc into each ch on 2nd row, make buttonholes on every foll 8th row until 40 rows of patt in all have been completed.

Shape armhole:

Cont to make buttonholes as before.

Next row: (RS) Patt to last 2[2:3] sts, turn.
Dec one st as before at armhole edge on next 5[6:6] rows. 19[21:22] sts. Work straight until 6th buttonhole has been completed (54[56:56] rows in total). Fasten off.

Shape neck:

Next row: (RS) Miss first 7[8:8] sts, rejoin yarn into next st, 2ch, dc2tog over next 2 sts, patt to end, turn.
Complete to match Left front neck shaping.

SLEEVES: (make 2)

With 8.00mm (UK 0) hook make 25[27:29]ch. Work foundation row as given for Back. 24[26:28] sts. Cont in patt as given for Back until 6[5:3] rows in all have been completed.

Inc row: 1ch, miss st at base of ch, 2dc into next st, patt to last 2 sts, 2dc into next st, 1dc into last st, turn. 1 st inc at each end of row. Cont to inc in this way at each end of every foll 7th[6th:6th] row until there are 38[42:46] sts. Work 5[6:2] rows straight. Fasten off.

Shape top:

Next row: (RS) Miss first 2[2:3] sts, rejoin yarn to next st, 1ch, 1dc into each of next 33[37:39] sts, turn. 34[38:40] sts.
Dec one st at each end of next 5[6:6] rows, then at each end of every foll alt row until 14[16:18] sts rem. Work 1 row, then dec one st at each end of every row until 8[8:10] sts rem. Fasten off.

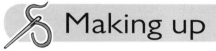

Making up

Dry press on WS with a warm iron.
Join shoulder seams. Set in sleeves, then join side and sleeve seams.

Sleeve edging:

With 7.00mm (UK 2) hook and RS facing, join yarn in seam of one sleeve, 1ch, 1dc into each st along cuff edge, join with a ss into first ch. *Do not fasten off, but with RS still facing and working from left to right, work 1dc into each st to form crab st edging. Fasten off.*

Outer edging:

With 7.00mm (UK 2) hook and RS facing, join yarn in left side seam, 1ch, 1dc into each st along edge of Back and Right front, 2dc into corner st, 1dc into alt row-ends of Right front, 2dc into corner st, 1dc into each st around neck, 2dc into corner st, 1dc into alt row-ends of Left front, 2dc into corner st, 1dc into each st along edge of Left front, join with a ss into first ch. Rep as given from * to * of Sleeve edging. Sew on buttons.

Handbag doorstop

Keep your door open on windy days with this nautical-style doorstop.

With its nautical-striped theme and colouring, this 'handbag-style' doorstop is made in chunky yarn and rows of double crochet and trebles. It will make an eye-catching feature when propping your door open.

GETTING STARTED

Quick and easy to work in chunky yarn but care is needed with making up for a good finish.

Size:
Finished doorstop is approximately 18cm (7in) wide x 19cm (7½in) high x 10cm (4in) deep, excluding handle

How much yarn:
2 x 100g (3½oz) balls of King Cole Magnum Chunky in colour A – French Navy (shade 179)
1 ball in each of colour B – Champagne (shade 10) and colour C – Rouge (shade 9)

Hook:
6.00mm (UK 4) crochet hook

Additional items:
4 x nautical-themed buttons
2 x Velcro dots
60 x 40cm (24 x 16in) piece of calico fabric
White sewing cotton and needle
Polyester toy filling
1kg (2lb) bag of rice or dried beans

Tension:
13 sts measure 10cm (4in) and 8 rows measure 9cm (3½in) over patt on 6.00mm (UK 4) hook
IT IS ESSENTIAL TO WORK TO THE STATED TENSION TO ACHIEVE SUCCESS

What you have to do:
Make front and back panels in stripes and alternate rows of double crochet and trebles. When working stripes, work over both ends (old and new) of yarn to save sewing them in later. Work side panel in one colour and same pattern. Work handle with central row of bobble stitches. Make lifebelt trim in rounds for front flap. Make up panels to resemble a handbag. Sew calico bag and use to weight doorstop.

The Yarn
King Cole Magnum Chunky (approx. 110m/120 yards per 100g/3½oz ball) is a mixture of 25% wool and 75% acrylic. It combines wool's good looks with the practical qualities afforded by man-made fibres and can be machine washed. There is a good colour range.

 Instructions

Abbreviations:

ch = chain(s); **cm** = centimetre(s) **cont** = continue; **dc** = double crochet **dc2tog** = (insert hook in next st, yrh and draw through a loop) twice, yrh and draw through all 3 loops on hook; **foll** = follows **rep** = repeat; **RS** = right side; **ss** = slip stitch **st(s)** = stitch(es);

tr = treble **tr2(4)tog** = (yrh, insert hook in next st, yrh and draw through a loop, yrh and draw through first 2 loops on hook) 2(4) times, yrh and draw through all 3(5) loops on hook; **WS** = wrong side **yrh** = yarn round hook

FRONT PANEL:

With 6.00mm (UK 4) hook and A, make 24ch.

1st row: (WS) 1dc in 2nd ch from hook, 1dc in each ch to end, turn. 23 sts.

2nd row: With A, 3ch (counts as first tr), miss st at base of ch, 1tr in each st to end, turn.

3rd row: With B, 1ch (does not count as a st), 1dc in each st to end, working last dc in 3rd of 3ch, turn.

4th–9th rows: Rep 2nd and 3rd rows 3 times.

10th row: With A, 3ch, miss st at base of ch, tr2tog over next 2 sts, 1tr in each st to last 3 sts, tr2tog over next 2 sts, 1tr in last dc, turn. 21 sts.

11th row: As 3rd row.

12th and 13th rows: As 2nd and 3rd rows.

14th row: As 10th row. 19 sts.

15th row: As 3rd row.

16th row: As 2nd row.

17th row: With A, 1ch, 1dc in each st to end. Fasten off.

BACK PANEL AND FRONT FLAP:

Work as given for Front panel to end, but do not fasten off.

Top piece:

18th row: (RS) As 3rd row.

19th row: As 2nd row.

20th–26th rows: Rep last 2 rows 3 times, then work 18th row again.

27th row: As 17th row.

Front flap:

28th row: With A, 3ch, miss st at base of ch, 1tr in back loop only of each st to end, turn.

29th row: As 3rd row.

30th row: As 10th row of Front panel. 17 sts.

31st row: With B, 1ch, 1dc in first st, dc2tog over next 2 sts, 1dc in each st to last 3 sts, dc2tog over next 2 sts, 1dc in 3rd of 3ch, turn. 15 sts.

32nd row: As 10th row of Front panel. 13 sts.

33rd row: With A, work in dc to end. Fasten off.

SIDE PANEL:

With 6.00mm (UK 4) hook and A, make 75ch. Cont in A throughout, work 1st–9th rows as given for Front panel. 74 sts. Fasten off.

HANDLE:

With 6.00mm (UK 4) hook and A, make 29ch. Cont in A throughout, work 1st–3rd rows as given for Front panel. 28 sts.

4th row: (WS) 3ch, miss st at base of ch, (tr4tog – make bobble – in next st, 1tr in each of next 4 sts) 5 times, make bobble in next st, 1tr in last st, turn.

5th row: As 3rd row.

6th row: As 2nd row.

7th row: As 3rd row. Fasten off.

LIFEBELT TRIM:

With 6.00mm (UK 4) hook and B, make 10ch, join with a ss in first ch to form a ring and work as foll: 3ch (counts as first tr), work 7tr in ring, 3ch, ss in ring, fasten off B; join C in ring, 2ch, ss in 3rd of 3ch in B, work 7tr in ring, 3ch, ss in ring, fasten off C; join B in ring, 2ch, ss in 3rd of 3ch in C, work 7tr in ring, 3ch, ss in ring, fasten off B; join C in ring, 2ch, ss in 3rd of 3ch in B, work 7tr in ring, ss in 3rd of 3ch in B, 2ch, ss in ring, fasten off C.

Making up

Fold side panel in half and mark midpoint on both long edges. Mark midpoint on lower edge of front panel. With WS facing, aligning midpoints and matching ends of side panel to top edge of front, pin side panel to front panel. With A, blanket stitch side edges in place and slip stitch along base.

Mark midpoint on back panel in same way and attach to other long edge of side panel in same way.

Match up ends of handle to side panels. Pin, then mattress stitch handle ends to bag. Fold handle in half lengthways and leaving 7 sts free at each end of handle, join edges.

Position two buttons as required on side panel and sew in place. Repeat on other side of bag. Sew lifebelt trim to centre of front flap. Position Velcro dots on WS of lower corners of front flap and corresponding positions on RS of front panel and sew in place.

Weight bag:
With pinking shears, cut two pieces of calico fabric 20 × 12cm (8 × 4¾in) for top and bottom and one piece 20 × 60cm (8 × 24in) for sides. With RS facing and taking 1cm (⅜in) seam allowance, sew short edges of side piece together to form a tube. With RS facing and taking 1cm (⅜in) turnings, sew one edge of tube around bottom piece. Repeat to sew top piece in place to other edge of tube, leaving one long edge open. Turn bag to RS. Partially fill bag with polyester filling, then place unopened bag of rice in position and top up with more filling, taking care not to overstuff. Fold in seam allowance on bag opening and slipstitch securely closed. Place weight bag into doorstop 'handbag' and close with Velcro fastening.

Mesh-pattern top

Slip this stylish crochet tunic over a vest top for the perfect summer cover up.

Featuring pretty picot edgings, this tunic-style sweater with flared sleeves in an openwork pattern, is drawn in at the waist with a band of half treble fabric.

GETTING STARTED

★★ *Mesh pattern is quite easy to keep correct but shaping and working neat edgings takes some practice.*

Size:
To fit bust: 86[91:97:102]cm (34[36:38:40]in)
Actual size: 94[98:104:108]cm (37[38½:41:42½]in)
Length: 65[66:67:68]cm (25½[26:26½:26¾]in)
Sleeve seam: 46[46:46:47]cm (18[18:18:18½]in)
Note: Figures in square brackets [ ] refer to larger sizes; where there is only one set of figures, it applies to all sizes

How much yarn:
12[13:14:15] x 50g (1¾oz) balls of Debbie Bliss Prima in Redcurrant (shade 06)

Hooks:
3.00mm (UK 10) crochet hook
4.00mm (UK 8) crochet hook

Tension:
20 sts and 10 rows measure 10cm (4in) square over main patt using 4.00mm (UK 8) hook
IT IS ESSENTIAL TO WORK TO THE STATED TENSION TO ACHIEVE SUCCESS

What you have to do:
Work main fabric in a simple openwork mesh. Pull in waist section by working in half treble fabric. Shape sleeves as described in instructions. Finish off neck, sleeve and lower edges with a picot edging.

The Yarn
Debbie Bliss Prima (approx. 106m/116 yards per 50g/1¾oz ball) is a natural yarn containing 80% bamboo and 20% extra fine merino. The fibres have a slight twist, and this gives good stitch definition. There are both bright and more subtle shades to choose from.

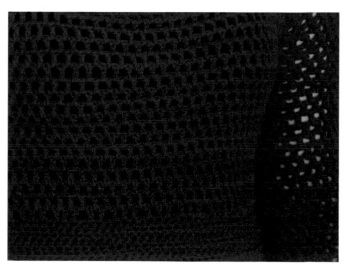

Instructions

Abbreviations:

alt = alternate
beg = beginning
ch = chain(s)
cm = centimetre(s)
cont = continue
dc = double crochet
dec = decrease(ing)
foll = following
htr = half treble
inc = increase(ing)
patt = pattern
rep = repeat
RS = right side
sp = space
ss = slip stitch
st(s) = stitch(es)
tr = treble(s)
WS = wrong side

BACK:

With 4.00mm (UK 8) hook make 97[101:107:111]ch.

Foundation row: (RS) 1tr in 6th ch from hook, *1ch, miss 1ch, 1tr in next ch, rep from * to last ch, 1tr in last ch, turn. 94[98:104:108] sts.

1st row: 4ch (counts as 1tr and 1ch), miss next st, 1tr in next 1ch sp, *1ch, 1tr in next 1ch sp, rep from * ending 1tr in turning ch, turn. The last row sets main patt.

Cont in patt until work measures 20cm (8in) from beg, ending with a WS row.

Dec row: 2ch (counts as 1htr), 1htr in each of next 5[5:5:6] sts, *miss next st, 1htr in each of next 2 sts, rep from * 26[27:29:30] times more, miss next st, 1htr in each of next 5[6:6:6] sts, 1htr in top of turning ch, turn. 66[69:73:76] sts.

Cont in htr for a further 7cm (2¾in), ending with a WS row.

Inc row: 2ch, 1htr in each of next 5[5:5:6] sts, *2htr in next st, 1htr in next st, rep from * 26[27:29:30] times more, 2htr in next st,

1htr in each of next 4[5:5:5] sts, 1htr in top of turning ch, turn. 94[98:104:108] sts.

Next row: 4ch, miss next st, *1tr in next st, 1ch, miss next st, rep from * to last 2 sts, 1tr in next st, 1tr in turning ch, turn.

Cont in main patt until work measures 43cm (17in) from beg, ending with a WS row.

Shape armholes:

Next row: Ss into each of first 7[7:9:9] sts, 4ch, patt to last 6[6:8:8] sts, turn. 82[86:88:92] sts.**

Cont in patt until armholes measure 21[22:23:24]cm (8¼[8½:9:9½]in) from beg. Fasten off. Mark centre 34[38:40:40] sts for back neck.

FRONT:

Work as given for Back to **.

Cont without shaping until armholes measure 6[6:7:7]cm (2¼[2¼:2¾:2¾]in) from beg, ending with a WS row.

Shape neck:

Next row: 4ch, miss next tr, *1tr in next

1ch sp, 1ch, miss next tr, rep from * 9[9:9:10] times more, 1tr in next 1ch sp, 1tr in next tr, turn.

Working on these 24[24:24:26] sts only, cont straight until armhole measures same as Back to shoulder. Fasten off. Return to sts at base of neck and leave centre 34[38:40:40] sts unworked, rejoin yarn to next st, 4ch, miss next tr, *1tr in next 1ch sp, 1ch, miss next tr, rep from * to last ch sp, 1tr in ch sp, 1tr in turning ch, turn. Cont straight until armhole measures same as Back to shoulder. Fasten off.

SLEEVES: (make 2)

With 4.00mm (UK 8) hook make 63[63:67:67]ch.

Foundation row: (RS) 1tr in 6th ch from hook, *1ch, miss 1ch, 1tr in next ch, rep from * to last ch, 1tr in last ch, turn. 60[60:64:64] sts.

1st row: 4ch, miss next st, 1tr in next 1ch sp, *1ch, 1tr in next 1ch sp, rep from * ending 1tr in turning ch, turn. The last row sets patt. Cont in patt, dec 1 st at each end of next and foll alt row. 56[56:60:60] sts. Work 4 rows straight. Now inc 1 st at each end of next and 2[7:7:13] foll alt rows (62[72:76:88] sts), then on 9[6:6:2] foll 3rd rows. 80[84:88:92] sts.

Cont without shaping until work measures 45[45:45:46]cm (17¾[17¾:17¾:18]in) from beg. Place a marker at each end of last row. Work 3[3:4:4] rows straight. Fasten off.

NECK EDGING:

Join shoulder seams.

With 3.00mm (UK 10) hook and RS of work facing, rejoin yarn to left shoulder, 1ch (counts as 1dc), work in dc evenly around neck edge so that there is a multiple of 3 sts + 1 extra, join with a ss to first ch, turn.

2nd round: 1ch, 1dc in each dc to end, join with a ss to first ch, turn. Work 2 more rounds in dc.

5th round: 1ch, *ss in next dc, 1dc in next dc, 3ch, 1dc in next dc, rep from * to end, join with a ss to first ch. Fasten off.

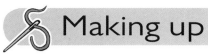

Making up

Join side seams. Join sleeve seams to markers. Sew in sleeves, sewing sts above markers to sts at underarms.

Lower edging:

With 3.00mm (UK 10) hook and RS of work facing, rejoin yarn to side seam, 1ch (counts as 1dc), work in dc evenly around lower edge so that there is a multiple of 3 sts + 1 extra, join with a ss to first ch, turn. Work 1 round in dc.

3rd round: Work as given for 5th round of Neck edging. Fasten off.

Sleeve edging:

Work as given for Lower edging.

Funky throw

A collection of motifs are sewn onto a plain mesh background to make this work-of-art throw.

Create this fantastic throw by stitching a selection of multi-coloured motifs to give an exciting pattern on to a simple mesh background with subtle stripes.

GETTING STARTED

★ ★ ★ *Individual elements are not difficult but assembly requires time and patience.*

Size:
Approximately 90cm (35in) square, without fringes

How much yarn:
Debbie Bliss Cashmerino Aran
3 x 50g (1¾oz) balls in colour A – Cream (shade 101)
2 balls in each of two colours: B – Grey (shade 009) and C – Beige (shade 102)
Debbie Bliss Cashmerino DK
2 x 50g (1¾oz) balls in each of six colours: D – Gold (shade 30); E – Black (shade 01); F – Russet (shade 35); G – Green (shade 11); H – Teal (shade 28) and I – Peacock (shade 33)

Hooks:
4.00mm (UK 8) crochet hook, 5.00mm (UK 6) crochet hook

Tension:
4 ch arches measure 9cm (3½in) and 12 rows measure 13cm (5in) over mesh patt on 5.00mm (UK 6) hook using Aran yarn
IT IS ESSENTIAL TO WORK TO THE STATED TENSION TO ACHIEVE SUCCESS

What you have to do:
Make throw in chain mesh pattern and stripes of three colours of Aran yarn. Work double crochet edging in DK yarn. Make all motifs in DK yarn and a selection of six colours. Motifs are a mixture of circular, square and hexagonal multi-coloured shapes. Sew motifs on to throw and add fringes.

Abbreviations:
beg = beginning; **ch** = chain(s) **cm** = centimetre(s) **cont** = continue **dc** = double crochet; **foll** = follows **htr** = half treble; **patt** = pattern **rep** = repeat; **RS** = right side **sp** = space; **ss** = slip stitch **st(s)** = stitch(es); **tr** = treble **tr2(3)tog** = (yrh, insert hook as directed and draw a loop through, yrh and draw through first 2 loops on hook) 2(3) times, yrh and draw through all 3(4) loops on hook **yrh** = yarn round hook

The Yarn
Debbie Bliss Cashmerino Aran for the throw (approx. 90m/98 yards per 50g/1¾oz ball) and Cashmerino DK for the motifs (approx. 110m/120 yards per 50g/1¾oz ball) both contain 55% merino wool, 33% microfibre and 12% cashmere. Luxurious yarns, they produce a soft finish ideal for a warm throw. There is a fantastic shade range of both.

 Instructions

THROW:
Note: Mesh pattern is worked in Aran yarn throughout and edging is worked in DK yarn.
With 5.00mm (UK 6) hook and A, make 162ch.
Foundation row: (RS) 1dc into 6th ch from hook, *5ch, miss 3ch, 1dc into next ch, rep from * to end, turn. 40 ch arches.
Patt row: *5ch, 1dc into next 5ch arch, rep from * to end, turn. Rep last row 10 times more.
Cont in patt as now set, working in stripes as foll: 12 rows B, 12 rows C, 12 rows A, 12 rows B, 12 rows C and 11 rows A.
Last row: With A, *3ch, 1dc into next 5ch arch, rep from * to end. Fasten off. Stretch mesh fabric gently so that all dc sts slip into centre of each 5ch arch.

Edging:
With 4.00mm (UK 8) hook and RS of work facing, join D to top right-hand corner.
1st round: 1ch, 1dc into first dc, *3dc into next ch sp, 1dc into next dc, rep from * all round, join with a ss into first dc.
2nd round: 1ch, 1dc into each dc all round, join with a ss into first dc. Fasten off.

MOTIFS:
Note: Worked in DK yarn only throughout.
Plain circle – 12cm (4¾in) diameter:
(make 1 in each of D, E, F, H and I)
With 4.00mm (UK 8) hook make 6ch, join with a ss into first ch to form a ring.

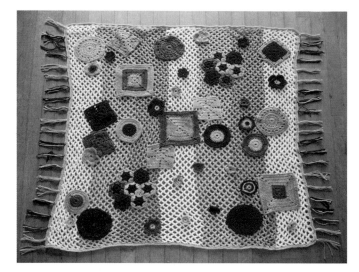

1st round: 3ch (counts as 1tr), 19tr into ring, join with a ss into 3rd of 3ch.

2nd round: 4ch (counts as 1tr, 1ch), (1tr into next tr, 1ch) 19 times, join with a ss into 3rd of 4ch.

3rd round: Ss into first ch sp, 3ch, 1tr into same place as ss, 2tr into each 1ch sp, join with a ss into 3rd of 3ch.

4th round: *4ch, miss 1tr, 1dc into next tr, rep from * all round, working last dc into first of 4ch.

5th round: Ss into first 4ch sp, 3ch, 2tr into same 4ch sp, *1ch, 3tr into next 4ch sp, rep from * all round, 1ch, join with a ss into 3rd of 3ch. Fasten off.

Striped circle – 10cm (4in) diameter:
(make 4, using 2 different colours for each as foll:
1. D for 1st contrast; I for 2nd contrast
2. G for 1st contrast; E for 2nd contrast
3. F for 1st contrast; G for 2nd contrast
4. I for 1st contrast; H for 2nd contrast)
With 4.00mm (UK 8) hook and 1st contrast, make 6ch, join with a ss into first ch to form a ring.

1st round: 3ch (does not count as a st), 12tr into ring, join with a ss into top of first tr.

2nd round: 3ch (does not count as a st), 2tr into each tr, join with a ss into top of first tr. 24 sts. Fasten off. Join in 2nd contrast to same place as ss on previous round.

3rd round: 3ch, (1tr into next tr, 2tr into next tr) 12 times, join with a ss into top of first tr. 36 sts.

4th round: 3ch, (1tr into each of next 2tr, 2tr into next tr) 12 times, join with a ss into top of first tr. 48 sts. Fasten off.

Bullseye circle – 6cm (00in) diameter:
(make 3 using a different colour of your choice for each round and joining in yarn each time in same place as final ss on previous round)

With 4.00mm (UK 8) hook and first colour, make 6ch, join with a ss into first ch to form a ring.

1st round: 1ch (does not count as a st), 8dc into ring, join with a ss into first dc. Fasten off.

2nd round: 1ch, 2dc into each dc, join with a ss into first dc. 16 sts. Fasten off.

3rd round: 1ch, 1dc in same place as join, (2dc in next dc, 1dc in foll dc) 7 times, 2dc in last dc, join with a ss into first dc. 24 sts. Fasten off.

4th round: 1ch, 1dc in same place as join, 1dc into next dc, (2dc in next dc, 1dc into each of next 2dc) 7 times, 2dc in last dc, join with a ss into first dc. 32 sts. Fasten off.

5th round: 1ch, 1dc in same place as join, 1dc into each of next 2dc, (2dc in next dc, 1dc into each of next 3dc) 7 times, 2dc in last dc, join with a ss into first dc. 40 sts. Fasten off.

Plain square – 10cm (4in): (make 1 in each of D, G, H and I;
make 1 using E for first 3 rounds and F for 4th round; make 1 using F for first 3 rounds and H for 4th round)
With 4.00mm (UK 8) hook, make 6ch, join with a ss into first ch to form a ring.

1st round: 3ch (counts as 1tr), 3tr into ring, 3ch, (4tr into ring, 3ch) 3 times, join with a ss to 3rd of 3ch.

2nd round: 5ch (counts as 1tr, 2ch), *miss next 2tr, 1tr into next tr, (2tr, 3ch, 2tr) into 3ch sp, 1tr into next tr, 2ch, rep from * twice more, miss next 2tr, 1tr into next tr, (2tr, 3ch, 2tr) into next 3ch sp, join with a ss into 3rd of 5ch.

3rd round: 5ch, *miss next 2ch sp, 1tr into each of next 3tr, (2tr, 3ch, 2tr) into 3ch sp, 1tr into each of next 3tr, 2ch, rep from * twice more, miss next 2ch sp, 1tr into each of next 3tr, (2tr, 3ch, 2tr) into next 3ch sp, 1tr into each of next 2tr, join with a ss into 3rd of 5ch.

4th round: 5ch, *miss next 2ch sp, 1tr into each of next 5tr, (2tr, 3ch, 2tr) into 3ch sp, 1tr into each of next 5tr, 2ch, rep from * twice more, miss next 2ch sp, 1tr into each of next 5tr, (2tr, 3ch, 2tr) into next 3ch sp, 1tr into each of next 4tr, join with a ss into 3rd of 5ch. Fasten off.

Large granny square – 14cm (5½in): (make 3 using G, H and I in different combinations as foll:
1. I for 1st and 2nd rounds, G for 3rd and 4th and H for 5th and 6th
2. G for 1st and 2nd rounds, H for 3rd and 4th and I for 5th and 6th
3. H for 1st and 2nd rounds, I for 3rd and 4th and G for 5th and 6th)
With 4.00mm (UK 8) hook and 1st colour, make 6ch, join with a ss into first ch to form a ring.

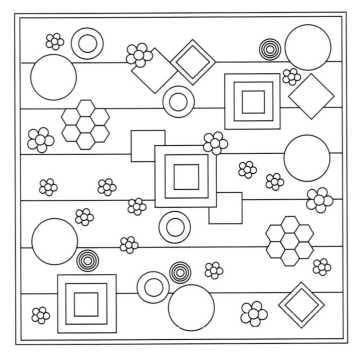

1st round: 5ch (counts as 1tr, 2ch), (3tr into ring, 2ch) 3 times, 2tr into ring, join with a ss into 3rd of 5ch.

2nd round: Ss into first 2ch sp, 5ch, (2tr into same 2ch sp, 1tr into each of next 3tr, 2tr into next 2ch sp, 2ch) 3 times, 2tr into same 2ch sp, 1tr into each of next 3tr, 1tr into first 2ch sp, join with a ss into 3rd of 5ch. Fasten off.

3rd round: Make a slip knot in 2nd colour and pull through 4th of 5ch at beg of previous round, 5ch (counts as 1tr, 2ch), (2tr into same 2ch sp, 1tr into each of next 7tr, 2tr into next 2ch sp, 2ch) 3 times, 2tr into same 2ch sp, 1tr into each of next 7tr, 1tr into first 2ch sp, join with a ss into 3rd of 5ch.

4th round: Ss into first 2ch sp, 5ch, (2tr into same 2ch sp, 1tr into each of next 11tr, 2tr into next 2ch sp, 2ch) 3 times, 2tr into same 2ch sp, 1tr into each of next 11tr, 1tr into first 2ch sp, join with a ss into 3rd of 5ch. Fasten off.

5th round: Make a slip knot in 3rd colour and pull through 4th of 5ch at beg of previous round, 5ch, (2tr into same 2ch sp, 1tr into each of next 15tr, 2tr into next 2ch sp, 2ch) 3 times, 2tr into same 2ch sp, 1tr into each of next 15tr, 1tr into first 2ch sp, join with a ss into 3rd of 5ch.

6th round: Ss into first 2ch sp, 5ch, (2tr into same 2ch sp, 1tr into each of next 19tr, 2tr into next 2ch sp, 2ch) 3 times, 2tr into same 2ch sp, 1tr into each of next 19tr, 1tr into first 2ch sp, join with a ss into 3rd of 5ch. Fasten off.

Hexagonal motif – 6cm (2½in) diameter:
(make 14 hexagons, using E for 1st round throughout and other colours as required)
With 4.00mm (UK 8) hook and E, make 6ch, join with a ss

into first ch to form a ring.

1st round: 3ch (counts as first tr), tr2tog into ring, 2ch, (tr3tog into ring, 2ch) 5 times, join with a ss in top of first tr2tog. Fasten off.

2nd round: Join in 2nd colour in first 2ch sp, (3ch, tr2tog, 2ch, tr3tog) in same 2ch sp as join, 4ch, (tr3tog, 2ch, tr3tog into next 2ch sp, 4ch) 5 times, join with a ss into top of first tr2tog. Fasten off.

Small flower: (make 2 in each colour)
With 4.00mm (UK 8) hook, make 6ch, join with a ss into first ch to form a ring.

1st round: 1ch, work 15dc into ring, join with a ss into first dc.

2nd round: (3ch, tr2tog over next 2dc, 3ch, ss into next dc) 5 times, working last ss into last dc of previous round. Fasten off.

Large flower: (make 5, using D for 1st round and then each of other 5 colours in turn)
With 4.00mm (UK 8) hook and D, make 6ch, join with a ss into first ch to form a ring.

1st round: 1ch, 10dc into ring, join with a ss into first dc. Fasten off.
Join in 2nd colour at same place as ss on previous round.

2nd round: 2ch, 2htr into each st to end, ss into first htr. 20htr.

3rd round: (2ch, working into front loop of st only, work 2tr into each of next 3htr, 2ch, ss into next htr) 5 times, working last ss into base of 2ch. Fasten off.

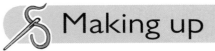 # Making up

Using diagram and picture as a guide, sew motifs on to mesh background. For circular motifs, work a few stitches at regular intervals around shape, cutting off and rejoining yarn each time. For square motifs, work a few stitches at each corner and in centre of each side in same way. For flowers, sew centre of each flower to a mesh chain space.

Fringe:
Alternating colours and using 1 strand of D with 2 strands of each of other colours of DK in turn, cut them into 25cm (10in) lengths. Starting in one corner, knot a coloured tassel every 8 sts along top and lower edges of throw. Trim to an even length.

Striped beach bag

Sashay along the sand in style with this bold striped bag.

This ideal summer bag, with thick cord handles, is brightly striped in a woven pattern and lined with an attractive fabric. It has colourful fish motifs attached to its handle with a twisted cord.

The Yarn

Debbie Bliss Eco Aran (approx. 75m/ 82 yards per 50g/1¾oz ball) is an aran-weight yarn containing 100% organic cotton. Produced within an ecological and socially conscious process, this beautiful yarn comes in a good range of natural and colourful bright shades.

GETTING STARTED

★★ *Woven pattern is straightforward to work but neat sewing is required to line basket for a professional finish.*

Size:
28 x 44cm (11 x 17¼in), excluding base

How much yarn:
Bag: 4 x 50g (1¾oz) balls of Debbie Bliss Eco Cotton in colour A – Orange (shade 601)
3 balls in colour B – White (shade 608)
Fish: Oddments of 4 ply yarn in fuchsia, orange and green (we used Debbie Bliss Baby Cashmerino)

Hooks:
Bag: 5.00mm (UK 6) crochet hook
Fish: 3.00mm (UK 11) crochet hook

Additional items:
1.4m (1½ yards) white cord for handles

4 x 14mm-diameter (#1) eyelets and washers
Lining fabric
Needle and matching sewing thread, Pencil
3 black seed beads for fish eyes
Small quantity of wadding

Tension:
9 patt reps and 16 rows measure 10cm (4in) square over woven patt on 5.00mm (UK 6) hook
IT IS ESSENTIAL TO WORK TO THE STATED TENSION TO ACHIEVE SUCCESS

What you have to do:
Work bag in broad stripes and woven pattern as instructed. Sew a fabric lining for bag. Insert eyelets at top edge as instructed for 'rope' handles. Crochet fish decorations in double crochet and attach to handles.

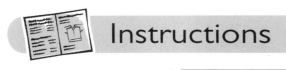

Instructions

Abbreviations:

ch = chain
cm = centimetre(s)
cont = continue
dc = double crochet
foll = follows
htr = half treble
patt = pattern
rep = repeat
RS = right side
sp(s) = space(s)
ss = slip stitch
st(s) = stitch(es)
tr = treble
WS = wrong side
yrh = yarn round hook

BEACH BAG:
Back:
With 5.00mm (UK 6) hook and A, make 82ch.

Foundation row: (WS) 1dc into 2nd ch from hook, *1ch, miss next ch, 1dc into next ch, rep from * to end, turn. 40 one-ch sps.

Cont in woven patt as foll:

1st row: (RS) 1ch, 1dc into first dc, 1ch, (insert hook into next ch sp, yrh and draw a loop through) twice, yrh and draw through all 3 loops on hook (cluster formed), *1ch, work a cluster inserting hook into previous ch sp and next ch sp, rep from * ending with 1dc into last dc, turn. 39 clusters.

2nd row: 1ch, 1dc into first dc, *1ch, 1dc into next cluster, rep from * ending with

1ch, 1dc into last dc, turn. 40 one-ch sps. These 2 rows form patt. Rep them twice more, then work 1st row again. Joining in and cutting off colours as required, cont in patt and stripe sequence of 8 rows B and 8 rows A until 3rd stripe in B has been worked. Patt 4 more rows in A. Fasten off.

Front:
Work as given for Back.

FISH DECORATION:
First side:
With 3.00mm (UK 11) hook and fuchsia, make 15ch.

1st row: (RS) Working into top loop only, work 1dc into 2nd ch from hook, 1dc into each of next 12ch, 3dc into last ch, then cont along other side of foundation ch, working 1dc into each of 13 loops along

other side of ch, turn.

2nd row: 1ch (counts as first dc), miss st at base of ch, 1dc into each of next 13dc, 3dc into next dc, 1dc into each dc to end, turn.

3rd row: 1ch, miss st at base of ch, 1dc into each of next 14dc, 3dc into next dc, 1dc into each dc to end. Fasten off.

Second side:
Work as given for first side but do not fasten off.

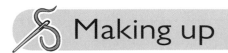

Making up

BEACH BAG:
Pin bag fabric out to size (this will help to correct slight bias of fabric), spray lightly with water and leave to dry. Using crochet as a template, cut two rectangles of lining fabric, allowing 1.5cm (⅝in) extra for seam allowances at each side edge and lower edge and 1cm (⅜in) at top edge for hem.

Join side seams of crochet bag, then join lower seam. With bag WS out, form base of bag into a rectangle and fold out corners. Measure 8cm (3in) from point and pin a line across corner; backstitch along line. Turn bag RS out and push out base of bag to form a bucket shape.

Make up lining fabric in same way. Trim seam allowances and press 1cm (⅜in) at top edge to WS. With WS together and seams matching, insert lining into bag and pin in place just below top edge. Slip stitch lining to bag around top edge. Mark position for eyelets between 12th and 13th patterns from side edges on first row of last stripe. Insert an eyelet through space in crochet fabric and mark its position in lining fabric with a pencil. Snip and remove a small area of fabric to take eyelet. Attach back of eyelet in place following manufacturer's instructions. Attach three more eyelets in same way. Cut cord in half and tie a knot in one end. Thread cord through one eyelet from front to back and out through other eyelet from back to front. Adjust length of handle and secure with a knot. Trim ends and untwist to form a tassel. Make another handle in the same way.

FISH DECORATION:
With WS together and working into both pieces, join two sides by working 1dc into each dc to centre, 3dc into centre dc, 1dc into each dc to end. Insert a small amount of wadding into fish, leaving 1.5cm (⅝in) free at top for tail, now work 3dc into first pair of row ends, 1dc into each of next 4 row ends, 3dc into last row end, join with a ss into first dc. Fasten off.

Fin:
Join yarn to 7th dc from tail, 3ch, 1tr into next dc, 1htr into each of next 2dc, 1dc into each of next 2dc, ss into next dc. Fasten off. Sew in ends. Gathering up fabric to form tail, wrap a length of yarn 3 times around fish 2cm (¾in) from tail end. Secure and sew in ends. Sew on a seed bead for eye. Make two more fish in same way using orange and green.

Tie:
Using two 70cm (28in) lengths of yarn in each of three colours, make a twisted cord. Tie a knot in loose ends only. Wrap cord around a handle and thread knotted end through looped end and draw up to secure tie to handle. Using one strand from each colour, attach centre of tail of each fish with a loop, securing end of yarn in knot on tie. Trim remaining ends to form a short tassel.

Bold striped cardigan

Blocks of colour are right on trend and this cardigan fits the bill perfectly.

With a boxy shape, set-in sleeves and buttoned to the neckline, this classic cardigan has three striking bands of colour across its body and sleeves.

GETTING STARTED

Simple double crochet and shaping but a neat fabric is essential for a good result.

Size:

To fit bust: 86[92:97:102]cm (34[36:38:40]in)
Actual size: 92[97:104:109]cm (36[38:41:43]in)
Length: 55[56:58:59]cm (21½[22:22¾:23¼]in)
Sleeve seam: 45cm (17¾in)
Note: Figures in square brackets [ ] refer to larger sizes; where there is only one set of figures, it applies to all sizes

How much yarn:

5[5:6:6] x 50g (1¾oz) balls of Debbie Bliss Rialto 4 ply in colour A – Charcoal (shade 04)
4[4:4:4] balls in colour B – Bright Pink (shade 22)
3[3:3:4] balls in colour C – Lavender (shade 20)

Hooks:

3.00mm (UK 11) crochet hook
3.50mm (UK 9) crochet hook

Additional items:

10[10:10:11] buttons

Tension:

25 sts and 22 rows measure 10cm (4in) square over patt when pressed on 3.50mm (UK 9) hook
IT IS ESSENTIAL TO WORK TO THE STATED TENSION TO ACHIEVE SUCCESS

What you have to do:

Work throughout in double crochet, working into back loop only of each stitch, and colours as directed. Follow instructions to shape armholes, neck and sleeves. Make buttonholes in right front edge. Work double crochet edging around front and neck edges.

The Yarn

Debbie Bliss Rialto 4 ply (approx. 180m/196 yards per 50g/1¾oz ball) contains 100% extra-fine merino wool. It produces a soft fabric with good stitch definition that can be machine washed at a low temperature. There is a comprehensive shade palette.

Instructions

Abbreviations:

alt = alternate
ch = chain(s)
cm = centimetre(s)
cont = continue
dc = double crochet
dc2tog = into each of next 2 sts work: (insert hook into st, yrh and draw through a loop), yrh and draw through all 3 loops on hook
dec = decrease(d)
foll = follow(s)(ing)
inc = increase(d)
patt = pattern
rem = remain
rep = repeat
RS = right side
st(s) = stitch(es)
WS = wrong side
yrh = yarn round hook

BACK:

With 3.50mm (UK 9) hook and A, make 117[123:131:137]ch.

Foundation row: (RS) 1dc into 3rd ch from hook, 1dc into each ch to end, turn. 116[122:130:136] sts.

Patt row: 1ch (counts as first st), miss st at base of ch, working into back loop only of each st throughout, 1dc into each st to end, working last dc into turning ch, turn. Rep last row 42 times more, ending with a WS row. Cut off A and cont in B for 36 rows, ending with a WS row. Cut off B.

Shape armholes:

Next row: (RS) Miss 5[5:6:6] sts, join C to next st, 1ch, miss st at base of ch, 1dc into each of next 105[111:117:123] sts, turn leaving 5[5:6:6] sts unworked. 106[112:118:124] sts. Cont in C.

Next row: 1ch, miss st at base of ch, dc2tog over next 2 sts, 1dc into each st to last 3 sts, dc2tog over next 2 sts, 1dc into turning ch, turn. 1 st dec at each end of row.

Rep last row 9[11:12:14] times more. 86[88:92:94] sts. Work straight for another 27[27:30:30] rows, ending with a WS row.

Shape back neck:

Next row: (RS) 1ch, miss st at base of ch, 1dc into each of next 27[28:29:30] sts, dc2tog over next 2 sts, 1dc into next st, turn and complete this side of neck first. Dec one st in from neck edge on next 5 rows. 25[26:27:28] sts. Fasten off.

With RS facing, miss centre 24[24:26:26] sts, rejoin yarn in next st, 1ch, miss st at base of ch, dc2tog over next 2 sts, 1dc into each st to end, turn. Complete to match first side of neck.

LEFT FRONT:

With 3.50mm (UK 9) hook and A, make 62[65:69:72]ch. Work foundation row as given for Back. 61[64:68:71] sts. Cont in patt and colours as given for Back to armhole shaping, ending with a WS row. Cut off B.

Shape armhole:

Next row: (RS) Miss 5[5:6:6] sts, join C to next st, 1ch, miss st at base of ch, 1dc into each st to end, turn. 56[59:62:65] sts.
Cont in C, dec one st in from armhole edge on next 10[12:13:15] rows. 46[47:49:50] sts. Work 15[15:16:16] rows straight, ending with a WS row.

Shape neck:

Next row: (RS) 1ch, miss st at base of ch, 1dc into each of next 32[33:34:35] sts, turn leaving 13[13:14:14] sts unworked.
Dec one st in from neck edge on next 8 rows. 25[26:27:28] sts. Work 9[9:11:11] rows straight. Fasten off.

RIGHT FRONT:

With 3.50mm (UK 9) hook and A, make 62[65:69:72] ch. Work foundation row as given for Back. 61[64:68:71] sts. Cont in patt and colours as given for Back, work 13[15:17:9] rows, ending with a WS row.
Buttonhole row: (RS) 1ch, miss st at base of ch, 1dc into each of next 2 sts, 2ch, miss 2 sts, 1dc into each st to end, turn. Working 1dc into each ch of buttonhole on next row, make a buttonhole on every foll 10th row until 36 rows in B have been completed, ending with a WS row. Cont in C, making buttonholes as before.

Shape armhole:

Next row: (RS) Patt to last 5[5:6:6] sts, turn. 56[59:62:65] sts.
Dec one st in from armhole edge on next 10[12:13:15] rows. 46[47:49:50] sts. Patt straight until 10th[10th:10th:11th] buttonhole has been completed, ending with a WS row.

Shape neck:

Next row: (RS) Cut off yarn, miss first 13[13:14:14] sts, rejoin yarn to next st, 1ch, 1dc into each st to end, turn. 33[34:35:36] sts.
Dec one st in from neck edge on next 8 rows. 25[26:27:28] sts. Work 9[9:11:11] rows straight. Fasten off.

SLEEVES: (make 2)

With 3.50mm (UK 9) hook and A, make 61[63:65:67]ch. Work foundation row as given for Back. 60[62:64:66] sts. Work 7[7:5:5] rows in patt as given for Back, ending with a WS row.
Next row: (RS) 1ch, miss st at base of ch, 2dc into next st, 1dc into each st to last 2 sts, 2dc into next st, 1dc into

turning ch, turn. 1 st inc at each end. Cont to inc one st at each end of every foll 6th[6th:5th:5th] row in this way until 62 rows in all have been completed, ending with a WS row. Cut off A.
Inc as before, cont in B until there are 88[92:98:102] sts. Work straight until 36 rows in B have been completed, ending with a WS row. Cut off B.

Shape top:

Next row: (RS) Miss 5[5:6:6] sts, join C to next st, 1ch, miss st at base of ch, 1dc into each of next 77[81:85:89] sts, turn leaving 5[5:6:6] sts unworked. 78[82:86:90] sts. Cont in C.
Next row: 1ch, miss st at base of ch, dc2tog over next 2 sts, 1dc into each st to last 3 sts, dc2tog over next 2 sts, 1dc into turning ch, turn.
Rep last row 9[11:12:14] times more. 58[58:60:60] sts. Now dec one st at each end of every foll alt row 6[6:7:7] times (46 sts), then at each end of every row until 32 sts rem.
Next row: 1ch, miss st at base of ch, (dc2tog over next 2 sts) twice, 1dc into each st to last 5 sts, (dc2tog over next 2 sts) twice, 1dc into turning ch, turn.
Rep last row once more. 24 sts. Fasten off.

Making up

Press pieces according to directions on ball band. With 3.00mm (UK 11) hook, C and RS facing, join shoulder seams with dc, working under 2 strands each time.

Edging:

With 3.00mm (UK 11) hook and RS facing, starting at lower edge of Right front, join A into first st, 1ch, *1dc into next row end, rep from * to last row end in A, change colour as foll: insert hook into next st, yrh with A and draw through a loop, yrh with B and pull through both loops on hook, making each colour change in this way, cont in B and then C to neck, 3dc into corner st, 1dc into each st or row-end around neck, then complete Left front to match, turn.
Next row: 1ch, 1dc into each st, making colour changes as before and working 2dc into centre st of 3dc at neck corners. Fasten off.
Sew in sleeves, then join side and sleeve seams. Sew on buttons.

Seaside cushion

Recreate a day by the sea with this bright picture cushion.

In this seaside scene the sky and sea background are worked in intarsia, then the rest of the motifs are made separately and sewn on. The cushion back resembles deckchair stripes.

GETTING STARTED

★★★ *Easy stitches but working from a chart requires practice and motifs must be neatly made and sewn on.*

Size:
50cm (20in) square

How much yarn:
1 x 100g (3½oz) ball of DMC Petra No.3 in each of seven colours: A – Variegated Blue (shade 54320); B – Sky Blue (shade 5798); C – Orange (shade 5722); D – Green (shade 5907); E – White (shade B5200); F – Red (shade 5666) and G – Yellow (shade 5742)

Hook:
3.50mm (UK 9) crochet hook

Additional items:
4 x12mm (½in) square buttons
50cm (20in) square cushion pad

Tension:
23 sts and 27 rows measure 10cm (4in) square over dc on 3.50mm (UK 9) hook
IT IS ESSENTIAL TO WORK TO THE STATED TENSION TO ACHIEVE SUCCESS

What you have to do:
Work cushion front mainly in double crochet and intarsia pattern from chart. Work cushion back in two pieces in coloured. stripes of double crochet and half trebles. Make separate appliqué motifs for cushion front. and sew in place. Add embroidered details.

The Yarn
DMC Petra No. 3 (approx. 280m/305 yards per 100g/ 3½oz ball) is a mercerized cotton yarn that produces a soft and supple fabric. It is ideal for crochet craft projects and there is a wide range of bright and pastel colours to choose from.

Instructions

Note: When working intarsia patt from the chart, read 1st and every foll alt (RS) row from right to left and 2nd and every foll alt (WS) row from left to right. Before you begin, wind off small, separate balls of yarn for each area of colour. When changing colours, complete final part of last st in old colour with new colour and loop yarns together on WS of work to prevent holes from forming.

FRONT:
With 3.50mm (UK 9) hook and A, make 111ch.
Foundation row: (RS) 1dc in 2nd ch from hook, 1dc in each ch to end, turn. 110 sts.
1st row: 1ch (does not count as a st), 1dc in each dc to end, turn.
Rep last row twice more, then cont in wave patt as foll:
Next row: 3ch (counts as first tr), working in back loop only of each st, work 1tr in st at base of ch, *1tr in each of next 2 sts, (tr2tog) twice, 1tr in each of next 2 sts, (2tr in next st) twice, rep from * to last 9 sts, 1tr in each of next 2 sts, (tr2tog) twice, 1tr in each of next 2 sts, 2tr in last st, turn.
Rep last row 6 times more. Cont in dc, work 9 rows straight.
Now cont in dc and intarsia patt from chart until all 100 rows have been completed. Fasten off.

BACK: (worked sideways; make 2)
With 3.50mm (UK 9) hook and G, make 61ch.
Foundation row: (WS) 1htr in 3rd ch from hook, 1htr in each ch to end, turn. 59 sts.
1st row: 2ch (does not count as a st), 1htr in each htr to end, turn.
Rep last row 6 times more, changing to E on last st.
Next 2 rows: With E, 1ch, 1dc in back loop only of each st to end, turn.
Cont in htr, work 6 rows in D and 2 rows in B.
Change to E and work 2 rows dc in back loop only of each st.
Cont in htr, work 2 rows in A and 6 rows in C.
Change to E and work 2 rows dc in back loop only of each st. Cont in htr, work 18 rows in F.
Now working stripes in reverse order as given before the 18 rows in F, patt 30 more rows. Fasten off.
Buttonhole border:
With 3.50mm (UK 9) hook and RS of work facing, join B

Abbreviations:
alt = alternate
beg = beginning
ch = chain(s)
cm = centimetre(s)
cont = continue
dc = double crochet
dc2tog = (insert hook in next st, yrh and draw a loop through) twice, yrh and draw through all 3 loops
dec = decrease(d)(ing)
foll = follow(s)(ing)
htr = half treble
inc = increase(d)(ing)
patt = pattern
rem = remain
rep = repeat
RS = right side
ss = slip stitch
st(s) = stitch(es)
tog = together
tr = treble(s)
tr2tog = (yrh, insert hook in next st, yrh and draw a loop through, yrh and draw through first 2 loops on hook) twice, yrh and draw through all 3 loops
WS = wrong side
yrh = yarn round hook

to corner of side edge of one back piece, 1ch (does not count as a st), work 105dc evenly along side edge (working 3dc in every 2 htr row-ends and 1dc in every 2 dc row-ends).
Work 1 row in dc.
Next row: 1ch, 1dc in each of next 20dc, (3ch, miss next 2dc, 1dc in each of next 19dc) 4 times, 1dc in last dc. Fasten off.

APPLIQUE MOTIFS:
Boat:
With 3.50mm (UK 9) hook and F, make 19ch.
Foundation row: (RS) 1dc in 2nd ch from hook, 1dc in each ch to end, turn. 18 sts.
1st row: 1ch (does not count as a st), 2dc in first dc, 1dc in each dc to last dc, 2dc in last dc, turn. 1st inc at each end of row. Cont in dc, inc at each end of every foll alt row until there are 26 sts.
Mast: Next row: 1ch, 1dc in each of next 13dc, make 20ch, 1dc in 2nd ch from hook, 1dc in each ch to end, ss in next dc on last row of boat, 1dc in

each dc to end. Fasten off.
Flag: With RS facing, join G to top dc on mast, 1ch, 1dc in each of first 4dc, turn and work 3 rows dc on these 4 sts.
Next row: 1ch, (dc2tog) twice. Fasten off.
First sail: With RS facing, miss next st of mast after flag and join E to next st on mast, 1ch, 1dc in each of next 13dc, turn.
Next row: 1ch, 1dc in each dc to last 2dc, dc2tog, turn. 1st dec at end of row.
Next row: 1ch, miss first dc, 1dc in each dc to end, turn. 1st dec at beg of row.
Rep last 2 rows until 3 sts rem.
Next row: 1ch, miss first dc, dc2tog. Fasten off.
Second sail: With RS facing and working on opposite side of mast, join E to 6th of starting ch for mast, 1ch, 1dc in each of next 13ch, turn.
Next row: 1ch, miss first dc, 1dc in each dc to end, turn. 1st dec at beg of row.
Next row: 1ch, 1dc in each dc to last 2dc, dc2tog, turn. 1st dec at end of row.
Rep last 2 rows until 3 sts rem.
Next row: 1ch, miss first dc, dc2tog. Fasten off.
Using picture as a guide, sew boat in position on left-hand side of front, with lower edge along last row of wave patt.
Kite:
Triangle panels: (make 1 in each of C, D, F and G)
With 3.50mm (UK 9) hook make 12ch. Work foundation row and 1st row as given for Front. 11 sts.
Next row: 1ch, miss first dc, 1dc in each dc to last 2dc, dc2tog, turn. 1st dec at each end of row.
Rep last row until 3 sts rem.
Next row: 1ch, miss first dc, dc2tog. Fasten off. Sew triangles tog to form kite. Sew in position to centre of left-hand cloud. With G and stem stitch, embroider a long curly tail onto end of kite.
Bows: (make 2 in each of D, C and F) With 3.50mm (UK 9) hook make 4ch. Work foundation row and 1st row as given for Front. 3 sts.

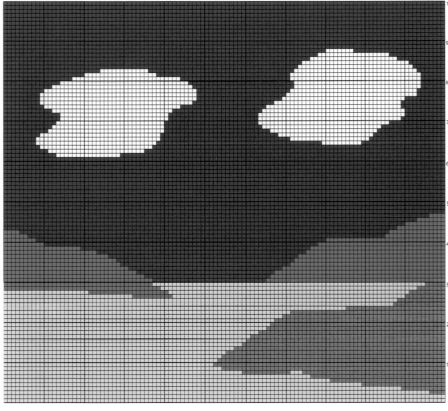

☐ A ■ B ■ C ■ D ☐ E

Next row: 1ch, miss first dc, dc2tog, turn.

Next row: 1ch, 3dc in dc2tog, turn. Work 1 row in dc. Fasten off. Sew bows onto kite tail.

Starfish:

With 3.50mm (UK 9) hook and G, make 4ch, join with a ss in first ch to form a ring.

1st round: 2ch (counts as 1htr), work 9htr in ring, join with a ss in 2nd of 2ch.

2nd round: 2ch, 1htr in same place as ss, (1htr in next htr, 3htr in next htr) 4 times, 1htr in next htr, 1htr in same place a ss, join with a ss in 2nd of 2ch. 20 sts.

3rd round: 2ch, 1htr in same place as ss, (1htr in each of next 3htr, 3htr in next htr) 4 times, 1htr in each of next 3htr, 1htr in same place as ss, join with a ss in 2nd of 2ch. 30 sts.

Working each point of star separately, cont as foll:

1st point: 1ch (does not count as a st), 1dc in each of first 6 sts, turn.

Next row: 1ch, miss first dc, 1dc in each dc to end, turn. Rep last row until 2 sts rem, turn and then work dc2tog and fasten off leaving a long tail.

2nd point: Rejoin yarn to next st, 1ch, 1dc in same st as join, 1dc in each of next 5 sts, turn. Complete as given for 1st point, then work 3rd, 4th and 5th points in same way.

Use long tails on each point to sew starfish in position on lower right-hand side of front.

Lighthouse:

With 3.50mm (UK 9) hook and F, make 27ch. Work foundation and 1st row as given for Front. 26 sts. Work 6 more rows in dc, joining in E at end of last row.

Working in stripes of 12 rows each E and F, cont as foll:

Dec row: 1ch (does not count as a st), miss first dc, 1dc in each dc to last 2dc, dc2tog, turn.

Work 5 rows straight. Rep last 6 rows until 12 sts rem. Cont in F. Work 8 rows straight.

Next 3 rows: 1ch, 2dc in first dc, 1dc in each dc to last dc, 2dc in last dc, turn. 18 sts.

Work 2 rows straight. Fasten off. With RS facing, miss first 4 sts, join G in next st, 1ch, 1dc in same st as join, 1dc in each of next 9 sts, turn.

Work 8 rows straight on these 10 sts. Change to F and work 1 row.

Next row: 1ch, miss first dc, 1dc in each dc to last 2dc, dc2tog, turn. Rep last row until 2 sts rem, then work dc2tog and fasten off.

Sew lighthouse in place to right-hand side of front. With B, work small cross stitches (over 1dc) to create door and windows. With B and backstitch, work railing along top of lighthouse. With E and long straight stitches held down with a small vertical stitch, add 3 seagulls to left of lighthouse.

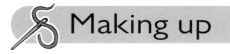

Making up

With RS facing, place two back pieces on front, overlapping piece without buttonhole edging over other piece. Join together around outer edges. Turn RS out and sew on buttons to correspond with buttonholes. Insert cushion pad and button closed.

Beach duffle bag

Swing into summer with this brightly coloured
bag over one shoulder.

Combining broad and narrow stripes in a colourful stitch pattern, this bag with its drawstring top is ideal for the beach. The interior has a simple sewn lining to make it practical and sturdy.

GETTING STARTED

★ ★ *Bag is worked in an easy stitch pattern but making up requires simple sewing skills for a good finish.*

Size:
Finished bag is 26cm (10¼in) in diameter across base x 43cm (17in) high

How much yarn:
1 x 100g (3½oz) ball of King Cole Bamboo Cotton DK in each of four colours: A – Green (shade 533; B – Peacock (shade 531); C – White (shade 530); D – Fuchsia (shade 536)

Hook:
4.00mm (UK 8) crochet hook

Additional items:
80cm (⅞ yard) of 90cm- (36in-) wide cotton fabric for lining
25cm (10in) square of heavyweight iron-on interfacing
Sewing needle and thread in white and colour to match lining fabric

Tension:
19 sts measure 10cm (4in) and 8 rows measure 7cm (2¾in) over patt on sides of bag on 4.00mm (UK 8) hook
IT IS ESSENTIAL TO WORK TO THE STATED TENSION TO ACHIEVE SUCCESS

What you have to do:
Work base of bag in rounds of half trebles, increasing as directed. Work sides in rounds of half treble pattern and stripes. Make eyelet holes for drawstring. Work pocket and straps in rows of double crochet. Sew fabric lining for bag and straps.

The Yarn
King Cole Bamboo Cotton DK (approx. 230m/251 yards per 100g/3½oz ball) contains 50% cotton and 50% bamboo. It makes a soft, strong fabric with clear stitch definition. There is a good range of colours.

Instructions

Abbreviations:

beg = beginning

ch = chain

cm = centimetre(s)

cont = continue

dc = double crochet

foll = follow(s)(ing)

htr = half treble

inc = increase

patt = pattern

rep = repeat

RS = right side

ss = slip stitch

st(s) = stitch(es)

WS = wrong side

BAG:

With 4.00mm (UK 8) hook and A, make 3ch.

1st round: 8htr in 3rd ch from hook, join with a ss in top of first htr.

2nd round: 2ch (do not count as a st), 2htr in st at base of ch, 2htr in each st to end, join with a ss in top of first htr. 16 sts.

3rd round: 2ch, 1htr in st at base of ch, (2htr in next st, 1htr in next st) 7 times, 2htr in last st, join with a ss in top of first htr. 24 sts.

4th round: 2ch, 1htr in st at base of ch, 1htr in next st, (2htr in next st, 1htr in each of next 2 sts) 7 times, 2htr in last st, join with a ss in top of first htr. 32 sts.

5th round: 2ch, 1htr in st at base of ch, 1htr in each of next 2 sts, (2htr in next st, 1htr in each of next 3 sts) 7 times, 2htr in last st, join with a ss in top of first htr. 40 sts.

6th round: 2ch, 1htr in st at base of ch, 1htr in each of next 3 sts, (2htr in next st, 1htr in each of next 4 sts) 7 times, 2htr in last st, join with a ss in top of first htr. 48 sts.

Cont in rounds as set, working one extra st between each inc, until foll round has been worked '2ch, 1htr in st at base of ch, 1htr in each of next 12 sts, (2htr in next st, 1htr in each of next 13 sts) 7 times, 2htr in last st, join with a ss in top of first htr. 120 sts.'

Next round: 2ch, 1htr in st at base of ch, 1htr in each st to end, join with a ss in top of first htr. Fasten off A.

Join C to same place as last ss and cont in patt as foll:

1st round: 2ch, 1htr in back loop only of st at base of ch, *1htr in front loop only of next st, 1htr in back loop only of next st, rep from * to last st, 1htr in front loop only of last st, join with a ss in top of first htr.

2nd round: 2ch, 1htr in front loop only of st at base of ch, *1htr in back loop only of next st, 1htr in front loop only of next st, rep from * to last st, 1htr in back loop only of last st, join with a ss in top of first htr.
The last 2 rounds form patt. Cont in patt, working in stripes of 6 rounds B, 2 rounds C, 6 rounds D, 2 rounds C, 6 rounds A, 2 rounds C, 6 rounds B, 2 rounds C and 6 rounds D.
Eyelet round: With C, 2ch, 1htr in back loop only of st at base of ch, patt 10 sts, (1ch, miss next st, patt 11 sts) 9 times, 1ch, miss last st, join with a ss in 2nd of 2ch. Patt 1 more round with C, then patt 6 rounds in A.
Last 2 rounds: With C, 1ch (does not count as a st), 1dc in each st to end, join with a ss in first dc. Fasten off.

STRAPS: (makes 2)
With 4.00mm (UK 8) hook and B, make 11ch.
Foundation row: 1dc in 2nd ch from hook, 1dc in each ch to end, turn.
Patt row: 1ch (does not count as a st), 1dc in each st to end, turn. 10 sts. Rep last row until Strap measures 76cm (30in) from beg. Fasten off.

POCKET: (worked sideways)
With 4.00mm (UK 8) hook and B, make 27ch. Work foundation and patt row as given for Straps. 26 sts. Cont in dc and stripe sequence of 4 more rows B, 2 rows C, 6 rows D, 2 rows C, 6 rows A, 2 rows C, 6 rows D, 2 rows C and 6 rows B, always joining in new colour on last part of last st in old colour. Fasten off.
Edging:
With 4.00mm (UK 8) hook, C and RS of work facing, join yarn to first row-end of one edge, 1ch, 1dc in each row-end to corner, turn. Work 1 more row in dc. Fasten off.

Making up

Lining:
Cut a 26cm- (10¼in-) diameter circle from cotton fabric and a 24cm- (9½in-)diameter circle from iron-on interfacing. Apply to centre of WS of fabric. Cut a 45 x 65cm (17¾ x 25½in) strip down length of fabric. Taking a 1cm (⅜in) seam allowance, join short ends to form an open tube. Now sew interfaced circle into one end of open tube. With WS facing, slip lining inside bag.

Fold raw edge of lining to inside and slip stitch in place around top edge, just below last 2 rounds of dc.
To make casing, work a row of small, neat running sts through base of sts of eyelet round. Work another row of running sts through top of sts on round above. With white sewing thread, work a row of running stitches through the middle of each white stripe on bag.
With C, make a twisted cord about 80cm (32in) long. Thread cord through eyelets so that ends emerge at centre front.
Sew pocket to centre front of bag as shown in photograph.
Cut a length of fabric 80cm (32in) long and 2cm (¾in) wider than straps. Cut in half widthways. Turn in raw edges of one piece and slip stitch in place to one end of strap, ending at centre. Turn strap over and sew second piece in place to other end of strap.
Sew centre of strap securely to centre back of bag, just below casing. Sew loose ends of straps securely to base of bag, approximately 20cm (8in) apart.

Sun hat with floppy brim

Pull on this floppy hat when the rays get too strong – it's perfect for snoozing in the shade.

Worked in an unusual cotton tape yarn, the crown and brim of this sun hat are worked separately and laced together with suede thong. The brim has an openwork, gently fluted effect.

The Yarn

Colinette Wigwam (approx. 130m/142 yards per 100g/ 3½oz ball) is a cotton tape yarn containing 100% cotton. Hand-wash only, it is available in an array of both variegated and solid shades.

GETTING STARTED

Easy stitches and shaping but care is needed with working in rounds.

Size:
To fit an average-sized woman's head

How much yarn:
1 x 100g (3½oz) hank of Colinette Wigwam cotton tape in Sea Breeze (shade 142)

Hooks:
5.50mm (UK 5) crochet hook
6.00mm (UK 4) crochet hook
7.00mm (UK 2) crochet hook

Additional item:
3mm- (⅛in-)wide suede thong

Tension:
16tr measure 10cm (4in) and 4 rounds of crown patt measure 5cm (2in) on 5.50mm (UK 5) hook
IT IS ESSENTIAL TO WORK TO THE STATED TENSION TO ACHIEVE SUCCESS

What you have to do:
Work crown in rounds of trebles, increasing as instructed. Work brim separately in rounds of trebles with chain spaces between them. Use different size hooks to shape brim. Lace crown and brim together with suede thong.

Instructions

Abbreviations:

ch = chain(s)

cm = centimetre(s)

cont = continue

dc = double crochet

foll = follows

patt = pattern

rep = repeat

sp(s) = space(s)

ss = slip stitch

tr = treble

WS = wrong side

Note:

To make a magic circle, wrap yarn clockwise around forefinger twice to form a ring. Holding end of yarn between thumb and middle finger, insert hook into ring and draw yarn from ball through.

CROWN:

With 5.50mm (UK 5) hook make a magic circle (see Note left).

1st round: 3ch (counts as first tr), work 11tr into ring, join with a ss in 3rd of 3ch. 12tr.

Gently pull on end of yarn to close magic circle.

2nd round: 3ch, 1tr into same place as ss, 2tr into each tr all round, join with a ss into 3rd of 3ch. 24tr.

3rd round: 3ch, 1tr into same place as ss, 1tr into next tr, (2tr into next tr, 1tr into next tr) all round, join with a ss into 3rd of 3ch. 36tr.

4th round: 3ch, 1tr into

same place as ss, 1tr into each of next 2tr,
(2tr into next tr, 1tr into each of next 2tr)
all round, join with a ss into 3rd of 3ch.
48tr.
5th round: 3ch, 1tr into same place as
ss, 1tr into each of next 3tr, (2tr into next
tr, 1tr into each of next 3tr) all round, join
with a ss into 3rd of 3ch. 60tr.
6th round: 3ch, 1tr into same place as
ss, 1tr into each of next 4tr, (2tr into next
tr, 1tr into each of next 4tr) all round, join
with a ss into 3rd of 3ch. 72tr.
Cont in crown patt as foll:
1st round: 4ch (counts as first tr and
1ch), miss next tr, 1tr into next tr, *1ch,
miss next tr, 1tr into next tr, rep from * all
round, ending with 1ch, join with a ss into
3rd of 4ch. 36 sps.
2nd round: 3ch, working into back loop
only, work 1tr into next ch, *1tr into next
tr, 1tr into next ch, rep from * all round,
join with a ss into 3rd of 3ch. 72tr.
These 2 rows form patt. Rep them twice
more. Fasten off.

BRIM:
With 5.50mm (UK 5) hook make 74ch.
Foundation round: 1tr into 4th ch
from hook, 1tr into each ch to end, join
with a ss into 3rd of 3ch to form a ring.
72tr.
1st round: 5ch (counts as first tr and 2ch), miss next
tr, 1tr into next tr, *2ch, miss next tr, 1tr into next tr, rep
from * all round, ending with 2ch, join with a ss into 3rd
of 5ch. 36 sps.
Change to 6.00mm (UK 4) hook.
2nd round: 5ch, 1tr into next tr, *2ch, 1tr into next tr,
rep from * all round, ending with 2ch, join with a ss into
3rd of 5ch.
3rd round: 6ch (counts as first tr and 3ch), 1tr into next
tr, *3ch, 1tr into next tr, rep from * all round, ending with
3ch, join with a ss into 3rd of 6ch.
Change to 7.00mm (UK 2) hook.
4th round: As 3rd round.
5th round: 7ch (counts as first tr and 4ch), 1tr into next
tr, *4ch, 1tr into next tr, rep from * all round, ending with
4ch, join with a ss into 3rd of 7ch.
Change to 5.50mm (UK 5) hook.

6th round: 1ch, 4dc into first loop, *1dc into next tr,
4dc into next loop, rep from * all round, join with a ss
into first ch. Fasten off.

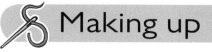

Making up

Sew in all ends. Using length of thong, oversew brim to
crown, working between pairs of trebles and butting
edges. Secure ends on WS. Pin out brim to size, spray
with clean water and leave until completely dry.

Zingy round cushion

Give your décor a colour pop with this bright circular cushion.

This circular cushion with a shell edging has stitches with a pronounced spiral effect and funky shaded colouring created by working with two strands of yarn.

The Yarn

Patons Diploma Gold DK (approx. 120m/131 yards per 50g/1¾oz ball) is a blend of 55% wool, 25% acrylic and 20% nylon. It combines wool's natural good looks with the easy-care properties of man-made fibres. It is machine washable, and there is a fantastic range of shades.

GETTING STARTED

★★ *Working in a spiral and frequent colour changes need constant attention.*

Size:
40cm (16in) in diameter

How much yarn:
2 x 50g (1¾oz) balls of Patons Diploma Gold DK in each of four colours: A – Orange (shade 06304); B – Cherry (shade 06139); C – Cyclamen (shade 06123); D – Violet (shade 06242)

Hook:
7.00mm (UK 2) crochet hook

Additional items:
40cm (16in) round cushion with red slip cover
Small safety pins

Tension:
First 3 rounds of front measure 10cm (4in) in diameter with two strands of yarn and 7.00mm (UK 2) hook (**Note:** subsequent rounds contract – every 4 rounds add 9cm (3½in) to diameter)
IT IS ESSENTIAL TO WORK TO THE STATED TENSION TO ACHIEVE SUCCESS

What you have to do:
Use two strands of yarn together throughout, changing colours at intervals to give a shaded effect. Work both sides of cushion in the round, starting at the centre and working in a continuous spiral. After cushion has been inserted, work a shell edging around outer edge.

Instructions

Abbreviations:
ch = chain(s)
cm = centimetre(s)
dc = double crochet
htr = half treble
rep = repeat
ss = slip stitch
st(s) = stitch(es)
tr = treble
yrh = yarn round hook

Notes:
Cushion is worked throughout using two strands of yarn together. Always join in new colour on last part of last st worked in old colour.

FRONT:
With 7.00mm (UK 2) hook and 2 strands of A, make 6ch, join with a ss in first ch to form a ring.

1st round: 2ch, 13tr in ring.

Note: In next and subsequent rounds, each st is worked around stem of tr rather than through two loops at top – work yrh, insert hook from back and from right to left around stem of tr and draw loop through, complete tr in usual way.

2nd round: 2tr in 2nd of 2ch, (2tr in next tr) 13 times, insert a small safety-pin in last st to mark end of round and move up on every round. 28tr.

3rd round: *2tr in next tr, 1tr in next tr *, rep from * to * twice more, cut off one strand of A and join in one strand of B, then rep from * to * to end. 42tr.

4th round: *2tr in next tr, 1tr in each of next 2tr, rep from * to end. 56tr.

5th round: *2tr in next tr, 1tr in each of next 3tr *, cut off strand of A and join in another strand of B, then rep from * to * to end. 70tr.

BACK:

Wrap two strands of D ten times round forefinger of left hand. Keeping hold of strands, remove 'ring' from finger, insert 7.00mm (UK 2) hook into ring, yrh and draw a loop through, 2ch, work 14tr into ring, pull gently on end of yarn to close up ring.

1st round: 2tr in 2nd of 2ch, (2tr in next tr) 14 times, insert a small safety-pin in last st to mark end of round and move up on every round. 30tr.

2nd round: *2tr in next tr, 1tr in next tr *, rep from * to * 3 times more, cut off one strand of D and join in one strand of C, then rep from * to * to end. 45tr.

3rd round: *2tr in next tr, 1tr in each of next 2tr *, rep from * to * 4 times more, cut off strand of D and join in another strand of C, rep from * to * to end. 60tr.

4th round: *2tr in next tr, 1tr in each of next 3tr *, rep from * to * 3 times more, cut off one strand of C and join in one strand of B, rep from * to * 3 times, cut off strand of C and join in one strand of A, rep from * to * to end. 75tr.

5th round: 1tr in each of next 40tr, cut off strand of B, join in another strand of A, 1tr in each tr to end.

6th round: *2tr in next tr, 1tr in each of next 4tr rep from * to end. 90tr.

7th round: 1tr in each of next 12tr, cut off strand of A and join in one strand of D, 1tr in each tr to end.

8th round: *2tr in next tr, 1tr in each of next 5tr *, rep from * to * 5 times more, cut off strand of A and join in another strand of D, rep from * to * to end (105tr), 1htr in next tr, 1dc in next tr. Fasten off.

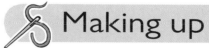

Making up

Pin front panel to one side of cushion and back panel to the other side. Holding edges with small safety-pins, slip stitch closed using one strand of yarn.

Edging:

With 7.00mm (UK 2) hook and front of cushion facing, join two strands of C to any tr, ss in same place as join, (miss next tr, 5tr in next tr, miss next 2tr, ss in next tr) to end. Fasten off.

6th round: *2tr in next tr, 1tr in each of next 4tr, rep from * to end. 84tr.

7th round: 1tr in each of next 35tr, cut off one strand of B and join in one strand of C, 1tr in each tr to end.

8th round: *2tr in next tr, 1tr in each of next 5tr, rep from * to end. 98tr.

9th round: 1tr in each of next 40tr, cut off strand of B and join in another strand of C, 1tr in each tr to end.

10th round: *2tr in next tr, 1tr in each of next 6tr, rep from * to end. 112tr.

11th round: 1tr in each of next 65tr, cut off one strand of C and join in one strand of D, 1tr in each tr to end.

12th round: 1tr in each tr to end.

13th round: *2tr in next tr, 1tr in each of next 7tr *, rep from * to * 4 times more, cut off strand of C and join in second strand of D, then rep from * to * to end. 126tr.

14th round: 1tr in each of next 2tr, cut off one strand of D and join in one strand of A, 1tr in each tr to end.

15th round: 1tr in each tr to end.

16th round: *2tr in next tr, 1tr in each of next 8tr *, rep from * to * 5 times more, cut off strand of D and join in second strand of A, then rep from * to * to end. 140tr.

17th round: 1tr in each of next 70tr, cut off one strand of A and join in strand of B, 1tr in each tr to end.

18th round: 1tr in each tr to end.

19th round: 1tr in each of next 10tr, cut off strand of A and join in second strand of B, 1tr in each tr to end (to marker pin), 1htr in next tr, 1dc in next tr. Fasten off.

Cobweb wrap

Mohair and silk combine to make the light and luxurious yarn for this stole.

Light as a feather and fluffy, this wrap is worked in a gorgeous mohair yarn and openwork pattern so that it resembles a cobweb.

GETTING STARTED

★ ★ *Straight strip of fabric but lace mesh pattern requires concentration.*

Size:
Wrap measures approximately 47 x 154cm (18 x 61in)

How much yarn:
3 x 25g (1oz) balls of Debbie Bliss Angel in Blue/ Green (shade 09)

Hook:
4.50mm (UK 7) crochet hook

Tension:
1 rep of patt measures 10cm (4in) across x 11cm (4⅜in) deep on 4.50mm (UK 7) hook
IT IS ESSENTIAL TO WORK TO THE STATED TENSION TO ACHIEVE SUCCESS

What you have to do:
Work throughout in lace mesh pattern incorporating motifs as directed. Work narrow edging around wrap.

The Yarn
Debbie Bliss Angel (approx. 200m/218 yards per 100g/1oz ball) is a blend of 76% superkid mohair and 24% silk. It produces a luxurious silky soft hand-wash fabric. There is a wide range of colours.

Instructions

Abbreviations:

ch = chain(s)

cm = centimetre(s) **cont**
= continue

dc = double crochet

foll = follow(s)(ing)

patt = pattern

rep = repeat

RS = right side

sp = spaces

ss = slip stitch

st(s) = stitch(es)

tr = treble

tr-tr = triple treble

tr-tr2tog = yrh 3 times,
insert hook in specified
st, *yrh and draw a loop
through, (yrh and draw
through first 2 loops
on hook) 3 times * (2
loops left on hook), yrh 3
times, insert hook in next
specified st, rep from *
to *, yrh and draw through
all 3 loops on hook

yrh = yarn round hook

WRAP:

With 4.50mm (UK 7)
hook make 76ch.

Foundation row: (RS)
1tr into 6th ch from
hook, (1ch, miss 1ch, 1tr
into next ch) 3 times,
*4ch, miss 1ch, tr-tr2tog
working first part of st
into next ch, then miss
3ch and work second
part of st into next ch,

4ch, miss 1ch, 1tr into next ch, (1ch, miss
1ch, 1tr into next ch) 4 times, rep from *
to end, turn.

Cont in patt as foll:

1st row: 4ch (counts as 1tr, 1ch), miss
first sp, 1tr into next tr, (1ch, miss 1ch, 1tr
into next tr) 3 times, *3ch, ss into top of tr-
tr2tog, 3ch, 1tr into next tr, (1ch, miss 1ch,
1tr into next tr) 4 times, rep from * to end,
working last tr into 4th of 5ch (and 3rd of
4ch for subsequent rows), turn.

2nd row: 4ch, miss first sp, 1tr into next tr,

(1ch, miss 1ch, 1tr into next tr) 3 times, *4ch, ss into ss, 4ch, 1tr into next tr, (1ch, miss 1ch, 1tr into next tr) 4 times, rep from * to end, working last tr into 3rd of 4ch, turn.

3rd row: 4ch, miss first sp, 1tr into next tr, (1ch, miss 1ch, 1tr into next tr) 3 times, *1ch, (1tr-tr, 3ch, 1tr-tr) into ss, 1ch, 1tr into next tr, (1ch, miss 1ch, 1tr into next tr) 4 times, rep from * to end, working last tr into 3rd of 4ch, turn.

4th row: 7ch (counts as 1tr, 4ch), miss first sp, tr-tr2tog working first part of st into next tr, then miss next tr and work second part of st into foll tr, 4ch, 1tr into next tr, *1ch, 1tr into next tr-tr, 1ch, 1tr into 2nd of next 3ch, 1ch, 1tr into next tr-tr, 1ch, 1tr into next tr, 4ch, tr-tr2tog working first part of st into next tr, then miss next tr and work second part of st into foll tr, 4ch, 1tr into next tr, rep from * to end, working last tr into 3rd of 4ch, turn.

5th row: 6ch (counts as 1tr, 3ch), ss into top of tr-tr2tog, 3ch, 1tr into next tr, *(1ch, miss 1ch, 1tr into next tr) 4 times, 3ch, ss into top of tr-tr2tog, 3ch, 1tr into next tr, rep from * to end, working last tr into 3rd of 7ch, turn.

6th row: 7ch (counts as 1tr, 4ch), ss into ss, 4ch, 1tr into next tr, *(1ch, miss 1ch, 1tr into next tr) 4 times, 4ch, ss into ss, 4ch, 1tr into next tr, rep from * to end, working last tr into 3rd of 6ch, turn.

7th row: 4ch (counts as 1tr, 1ch), (1tr-tr, 3ch, 1tr-tr) into ss, 1ch, 1tr into next tr, *(1ch, miss 1ch, 1tr into next tr) 4 times, 1ch, (1tr-tr, 3ch, 1tr-tr) into ss, 1ch, 1tr into next tr, rep from * to end, working last tr into 3rd of 7ch, turn.

8th row: 4ch (counts as 1tr, 1ch), 1tr into tr-tr, 1ch, 1tr into 2nd of next 3ch, 1ch, 1tr into next tr-tr, 1ch, 1tr into next tr, *4ch, tr-tr2tog working first part of st into next tr, then miss next tr and work second part of st into foll tr, 4ch, 1tr into next tr, 1ch, 1tr into tr-tr, 1ch, 1tr into 2nd of next 3ch, 1ch, 1tr into next tr-tr, 1ch, 1tr into next tr, rep from * to end, working last tr into 3rd of 4ch, turn.

The last 8 rows form patt. Rep them 11 times more, then work 1st to 3rd rows again (wrap should measure 138cm/54in). Turn at end of last row but do not fasten off.

Edging:

1st round: 1dc into each st along top edge, 3dc into first row end, 2dc into each row-end down first side, 1dc into each ch along lower edge, 3dc into first row end, 1dc into each row end up second side, join with a ss into first dc.

2nd round: 3ch (counts as first tr), 1tr into next dc, *(1ch, miss 1dc, 1tr into each of next 2dc) to next corner, 3ch, 1tr into each of next 2dc, rep from * 3 times more omitting 2tr at end of last rep, join with a ss into 3rd of 3ch. Fasten off.

Bead-trimmed beach bag

Nautical colours and bright zingy beads make this bag a great summertime accessory.

Lined and with 'rope' handles, this bag is worked in double crochet and straw-coloured and white stripes, with side pockets in turquoise and white. The top edge and pockets are trimmed with beaded string tassels.

GETTING STARTED

★★ *Bag is easy to make but sewing skills are needed for making lining and adding neat finishing touches.*

Size:
Finished size, when standing, approximately 30cm (12in) wide x 30cm (12in) high, excluding handles

How much yarn:
4 x 50g (1¾oz) balls of Debbie Bliss Eco Aran in colour A – Straw (shade 603)
3 balls in colour B – White (shade 617)
1 ball in colour C – Turquoise (shade 622)

Hooks:
4.50mm (UK 7) crochet hook
5.00mm (UK 6) crochet hook

Additional items:
Stitch markers
60cm (24in) of thick piping cord
1 small roll of natural jute garden string
Assorted wooden beads
50cm (⅝ yard) of 90cm- (36in-) wide cotton lining fabric
50cm (⅝ yard) of 90cm- (36in-) wide heavy, sew-in fabric stiffener
Matching sewing thread

Tension:
15 sts and 17 rows measure 10cm (4in) square over dc on 5.00mm (UK 6) hook
IT IS ESSENTIAL TO WORK TO THE STATED TENSION TO ACHIEVE SUCCESS

What you have to do:
Work bag in one piece in rows of double crochet and stripes in two colours. Make one large and two small striped pockets for bag. Make handles using string and double crochet worked over piping cord. Sew fabric lining for bag. Decorate top of bag and buttonholes on pockets with string tassels threaded with beads.

The Yarn
Debbie Bliss Eco Aran (approx. 75m/82 yards per 50g/1¾oz ball) contains 100% organic cotton. It has a matt finish and is machine washable. There is a wide range of colours.

Instructions

Abbreviations:

ch = chain(s)
cm = centimetre(s)
cont = continue
dc = double crochet
patt = pattern
rep = repeat
RS = right side
ss = slip stitch
st(s) = stitch(es)
tr = treble
WS = wrong side

BAG:

With 5.00mm (UK 6) hook and A, make 61 ch.

Foundation row: (RS) 1 dc into 2nd ch from hook, 1 dc into each ch to end, turn. 60 sts.

1st row: 1 ch (does not count as a st), 1 dc into each dc to end, turn. Rep last row twice more, changing to B on last part of last st in A. Cont in rows of dc and stripe patt of 2 rows B and 4 rows A until 50 rows in all have been completed.

Shape base:

Next row: Ss into each of first 8 dc, 1 dc into each of next 44 dc, turn.

Cont in stripe patt as set for a further 8 rows. Place a marker at each end of last row. Cont in stripe patt for 8 more rows.

Next row: 9 ch, 1 dc into 2nd ch from hook, 1 dc into each of next 7 ch, 1 dc into each dc to end, turn. Rep last row once more. 60 sts. Cont in stripe patt for a further 49 rows. Fasten off.

BIG POCKET:

With 5.00mm (UK 6) hook and C, make 31 ch.

** **Foundation row:** (RS) 1 dc into 2nd ch from hook, 1 dc into each ch to end, turn.

1st row: 1 ch (does not count as a st), 1 dc into each dc to end, turn. Cont in rows of dc and stripe patt of 2 rows B and 4 rows C until 23 rows in all

Making up

Lay bag out flat and cut heavy, sew-in fabric stiffener to same size. Using stiffener as a template, cut out cotton lining fabric to same size, adding 1cm (⅜in) all round for seam allowance. Join side seams on bag. Join base seams by placing row-end markers to side seams and joining two edges together. Oversew side and base edges of fabric stiffener to match. Make up fabric lining in same way as bag, taking 1cm (⅜in) seam allowance. Fold 1cm (⅜in) around top edge to WS and press in place.

Upper edging:
With 4.50mm (UK 7) hook and RS of work facing, join C to one side seam at top edge, 1ch, 1dc into each dc or foundation ch around upper edge of bag, join with a ss into first dc.

Next round: 1ch, 1dc into each dc to end, join with a ss into first dc. Fasten off. Sew big pocket centrally to one side of bag, placing top stripe in B on pocket level with 3rd stripe in B down from top edge. Sew two small pockets to other side of bag in same way, leaving a 4cm (1½in) gap between them. Sew large beads for buttons on to bag corresponding with chain loops on pockets. Cut piping cord in half to make two handles and sew securely to inside of bag, 2cm (¾in) down from top edge (these joins will be covered by linining).

Handles:
Secure one end of string with sewing thread to piping cord at right-hand end and use string to work tightly spaced dc along length of handles. Fasten off. Secure string again at opposite end.

Fringe:
Cut 27 x 20cm (8in) lengths of string. Knot a fringe through each pocket, just below buttonhole. Use remaining 24 lengths of string to make a fringe around top edge of bag just below 2 rows of contrast edging and placing them 5 sts apart. Thread assorted wooden beads onto all ends of fringe, securing in place with a small knot. Slip fabric stiffener into bag and then, with WS facing, place lining into bag and slip stitch in position around top edge, just below top round of contrast edging.

have been completed. **
Next row: 1ch, 1dc into each of first 14dc, 2ch, miss next 2dc, 1dc into each dc to end. Fasten off.

SMALL POCKET: (make 2)
With 5.00mm (UK 6) hook and C, make 15ch. Work as given for Big pocket from ** to **.
Next row: 1ch, 1dc into each of first 6dc, 2ch, miss next 2dc, 1dc into each dc to end. Fasten off.

Waterfall jacket

This simple yet stylish jacket has a real designer look.

Worked in a soft and luxurious yarn, this easy-to-wear jacket has a rib-effect collar that folds back and forms long, pointed edges at the front.

The Yarn
Rowan Lima (approx. 110m/120 yards per 50g/1¾oz ball) is a blend of 84% alpaca, 8% merino wool and 8% nylon. This luxurious yarn is fairly chunky and has an unusual chain construction. There are natural and deep shades.

 Instructions

Abbreviations:
beg = beginning **ch** = chain **cm** = centimetre(s) **cont** = continue **dc** = double crochet **dec** = decrease **inc** = increase **patt** = pattern **rem** = remaining **rep** = repeat **rtrb** = relief treble back: inserting hook from right to left and from back to front, work 1tr around stem of st indicated **rtrf** = relief treble front: inserting hook from right to left and from front to back, work 1tr around stem of st indicated **RS** = right side **st(s)** = stitch(es) **tr** = treble **tr2(3)tog** = work 1tr into each of next 2(3) sts as indicated leaving last loop of each on hook, yrh and draw through all 3(4) loops **WS** = wrong side **yrh** = yarn round hook

JACKET LEFT HALF:
(Worked from centre back outwards to sleeve edge). With 5.00mm (UK 6) hook make 98[100:102]ch.

GETTING STARTED

★★★ *Although worked in a basic stitch, this large jacket has a lot of shaping.*

Size:
To fit bust: 81–86[91–96:101–106]cm (32–34 [36–38:40–42]in)
Actual size: 93[102:111]cm (36½[40:43½]in)
Back length: 62[63:64]cm (24½[24¾:25¼]in)
Length from centre back to cuff: 65[67:69]cm (25½[26½:27]in)
Note: Figures in square brackets [ ] refer to larger sizes; where there is only one set of figures, it applies to all sizes
How much yarn:
20[22:25] x 50g (1¾oz) balls of Rowan Lima in Chile (shade 882)

Hooks:
4.50mm (UK 7) crochet hook
5.00mm (UK 6) crochet hook
Tension:
16 sts and 9 rows measure 10cm (4in) square over tr on 5.00mm (UK 6) hook
IT IS ESSENTIAL TO WORK TO THE STATED TENSION TO ACHIEVE SUCCESS
What you have to do:
Make jacket in two halves, working each half from centre back towards sleeve edge. Work in trebles for main fabric, shaping as directed. Work collar and cuffs in raised treble rib.

Foundation row: (RS) 1tr in 4th ch from hook, 1tr in each ch to end, turn. 96[98:100] sts.

Patt row: 3ch (counts as first tr), miss st at base of ch, 1tr in each st to end, working last tr in 3rd of 3ch, turn. Rep last row twice more. **

Shape back neck:

1st neck row: (RS) 3ch, miss st at base of ch, 2tr in next st, 1tr in each st to end, working last tr in 3rd of 3ch, turn.

2nd neck row: 3ch, miss st at base of ch, 1tr in each st to last 2 sts, 2tr in next st, 1tr in 3rd of 3ch, turn. 98[100:102] sts.

Shape front edge:

Next row: (RS) Make 118[121:124]ch, tr2tog over 4th and 5th ch from hook, 1tr in each of rem 113[116:119] ch, 1tr in each tr to end, working last tr in 3rd of 3ch, turn. 213[218:223] sts.

WS dec row: 3ch, miss st at base of ch, 1tr in each st to last 3 sts, tr2tog over next 2 sts, 1tr in 3rd of 3ch, turn.

RS dec row: 3ch, miss st at base of ch, tr2tog over next 2 sts, 1tr in each tr to end, working last tr in 3rd of 3ch, turn. 211[216:221] sts. Rep last 2 rows 5 more times, then work WS dec row again. 200[205:210] sts. Work 1 row straight, then work WS dec row. Rep last 2 rows 1[2:3] more times. 198[202:206] sts; 24[26:28] rows in all. Fasten off.

*** Sleeve:

1st sleeve row: Rejoin yarn to 42nd[43rd:44th] st of previous row, 3ch, miss st at base of ch, tr3tog over next 3 sts, 1tr in each of next 108[110:112] sts, tr3tog over next 3 sts, 1tr in next st, turn leaving 41[42:43] sts unworked. 112[114:116] sts.

2nd sleeve row: 3ch, miss st at base of ch, tr3tog over next 3 sts, 1tr in each st to last 4 sts, tr3tog over next 3 sts, 1tr in 3rd of 3ch, turn. 108[110:112] sts.
Rep last row 6 more times. 84[86:88] sts; 8 sleeve rows.

9th sleeve row: 3ch, miss st at base of ch, tr2tog over next 2 sts, 1tr in each st to last 3 sts, tr2tog over next 2 sts, 1tr in 3rd of 3ch, turn. 82[84:86] sts. Rep last row 11 more times. 60[62:64] sts; 20 sleeve rows.
Work 1 row straight, then work 9th sleeve row again. Rep last 2 rows 3 more times. 52[54:56] sts; 28 sleeve rows. Work straight until length from centre back measures 62.5[64.5:66.5]cm (24½[25½:26¼]in) (or 2.5cm /1in less than length required), ending with a WS row.

Cuff:

Change to 4.50mm (UK 7) hook.

1st rib row: (RS) 2ch, miss st at base of ch, tr2tog over next 2 sts, 1tr in each st, ending 1tr in 3rd of 3ch, turn. 51[53:55] sts.

2nd rib row: 2ch, miss st at base of ch, *1rtrb around next st, 1rtrf around next st, rep from * to last 2 sts, 1rtrb around next st, 1tr in 2nd of 2ch, turn.

3rd rib row: 2ch, miss st at base of ch, *1rtrf around next st, 1rtrb around next st, rep from * to last 2 sts, 1rtrf around next st, 1tr in 2nd of 2ch. Fasten off.

JACKET RIGHT HALF:

Work as given for Left half to **.

Shape back neck:

1st neck row: (RS) 3ch, miss st at base of ch, 1tr in each st to last 2 sts, 2tr in next st, 1tr in 3rd of 3ch, turn.

2nd neck row: 3ch, miss st at base of ch, 2tr in next st, 1tr in each st to end, working last tr in 3rd of 3ch, turn. 98[100:102] sts.

Shape front edge:

Using separate ball of yarn, join to beg of previous row and make 116[119:122]ch. Fasten off.

Next row: (RS) 3ch, miss st at base of ch, 1tr in each tr to end, 1tr in each ch to last 3ch, tr2tog over next 2ch, 1tr in last ch, turn. 213[218:223] sts.

WS dec row: 3ch, miss st at base of ch, tr2tog over next 2 sts, 1tr in each tr to end, working last tr in 3rd of 3ch, turn.

RS dec row: 3ch, miss st at base of ch, 1tr in each st to last 3 sts, tr2tog over next 2 sts, 1tr in 3rd of 3ch, turn. 211[216:221] sts. Rep last 2 rows 5 more times, then work WS dec row again. 200[205:210] sts.
Work 1 row straight, then work WS dec row. Rep last 2 rows 1[2:3] more times. 198[202:206] sts; 24[26:28] rows in all. Fasten off.
Complete as given for Left half from *** to end.

COLLAR:

Join centre back seam. With 4.50mm (UK 7) hook and RS facing, join yarn to base of first ch at right front lower corner, 1ch, 1dc in base of each of 116[119:122]ch up front edge, 2dc in side edge of each of 6 rows to centre back seam, 2dc in side edge of each of next 6 rows and 1dc in base of each of 116[119:122]ch, ending at left front corner. 256[262:268] sts.

Shape collar stand:

1st row: 1ch (counts as first dc), miss st at base of ch, 1dc in each of next 157[160:163] sts, turn. 158[161:164] sts.

2nd row: 1ch, miss st at base of ch, 1dc in each of next 59 sts, turn. 60 sts.

3rd row: 1ch, miss st at base of ch, 1dc in each of next 59 sts, 1dc in each of next 6 sts of 1st row, turn. 66 sts.

4th row: 1ch, miss st at base of ch, 1dc in each of next 65 sts, 1dc in each of next 6 sts of 1st row, turn. 72 sts.

5th row: 1ch, miss st at base of ch, 1dc in each of next 71 sts, 1dc in each st of 1st row to end, turn.

Inc row: 3ch, miss st at base of ch, 1tr in each of next 7[10:13] sts, *2tr in next st, 1tr in each of next 4 sts, rep from * to last 8[11:14] sts, 2tr in next st, 1tr in each of next 6[9:12] sts, 1tr in 1ch, turn. 305[311:317] sts.
Rep 2nd and 3rd rib rows as given for Cuff until Collar measures 5cm (2in) (omitting collar-stand rows).
Change to 5.00mm (UK 6) hook. Cont in rib until Collar measures 15[16:17]cm (6[6¼:6¾]in). Fasten off.

Making up

Join side and sleeve seams. With 4.50mm (UK 7) hook and RS facing, join yarn at lower left front collar, 1ch, 3dc in side edge of every 2 rib rows and 2dc in side edge of every tr row all along lower edge, ending at lower right front collar corner. Fasten off. Press according to directions on ball band, omitting ribbing.

Work-of-art scarf

Let your creativity run riot with this stunning scarf.

Stand out from the crowd with this eye-catching scarf worked in a colourful variegated yarn and mesh pattern. The ends have a fantastic fringe comprising beaded floral and spiral motifs and ribbon tassels.

The Yarn
Noro Kureyon
(approx. 100m/
109 yards per
50g/1¾oz ball) is
a hand-dyed 100%
wool yarn. Hand-
wash only, in vivid
striped colours.

GETTING STARTED

 Scarf and embellishments are easy to make.

Size:
Scarf measures 22 x 210cm (8½ x 83in), excluding fringe

How much yarn:
5 x 50g (1¾oz) balls of Noro Kureyon in shade 226

Hook:
5.00mm (UK 6) crochet hook

Additional items:
Oddments of double knitting yarn in brick red and rust
Glass pony beads (with large holes) in brick red and lime green

1m (1 yard) of 15mm- (⅝in) wide sheer ribbon in chartreuse, brick and bottle green

Tension:
16 sts measure 10cm (4in) and 10 rows measure 11cm (4¼in) over basic mesh patt on 5.00mm (UK 6) hook
IT IS ESSENTIAL TO WORK TO THE STATED TENSION TO ACHIEVE SUCCESS

What you have to do:
Make scarf in main yarn and basic mesh pattern. Crochet embellishments – spirals and flower motifs – in a variety of colours. Decorate ends of scarf with embellishments, adding ribbon and yarn fringes.

Instructions

SCARF:
With 5.00mm (UK 6) hook make 37ch.

Foundation row: (RS) 1tr into 4th ch from hook, 1tr into each ch to end, turn. 35 sts.

1st row: 3ch (counts as first tr), miss st at base of ch, 1tr into each of next 2 sts, *1ch, miss next st, 1tr into each of next 3 sts, rep from * to end, working last tr into 3rd of 3ch, turn.

2nd row: 3ch, miss st at base of ch, 1tr into next st, *1ch, miss next st, 1tr into 1ch sp, 1ch, miss next st, 1tr into next st, rep from * to last st, 1tr into 3rd of 3ch, turn. 16 ch sps plus 2tr at each end.

3rd–6th rows: 3ch, miss st at base of ch, 1tr into next st, *1ch, miss next ch sp, 1tr into next st, rep from * to end, 1tr into 3rd of 3ch, turn.

7th row: 3ch, miss st at base of ch, 1tr into next st, 1tr into next ch sp, *1ch, miss next st, 1tr into each of next ch sp, next st and foll ch sp (3tr), rep from * to end, working last tr into 3rd of 3ch, turn.

8th row: 3ch, miss st at base of ch, 1tr into each st and ch sp to end, working last tr into 3rd of 3ch, turn. 35 sts.

9th and 10th rows: As 1st and 2nd rows. Cont in basic mesh patt as given for 3rd row until Scarf measures 190cm (75in)

end. Twist finished strip into a spiral.

Irish crochet flower: (make 7)

With 5.00mm (UK 6) hook and first colour, make 7ch, join with a ss into first ch to form a ring.

1st round: 1ch (counts as first dc), work 11dc into ring, join with a ss into first ch.**

2nd round: 3ch, miss st at base of ch and next st, 1dc into next st, *2ch, miss next st, 1dc into next st, rep from * 3 times more, 2ch, miss next st, join with a ss into first of 3ch. Fasten off.

3rd round: Join second colour to any 2ch sp, into each 2ch sp work (1ss, 1htr, 1tr, 1dtr, 1tr, 1htr and 1ss). Fasten off.

Fluffy flower: (make 2)

Work as given for Irish crochet flower to **. Fasten off.

2nd round: Join second colour to any dc, *7ch, 1dc into next st, rep from * to end. Fasten off.

Hanging flower: (make 4)

Thread 3 beads onto yarn. With 5.00mm (UK 6) hook and beaded yarn, make 5ch, join with a ss into first ch to form a ring.

1st round: *(1ch, 1htr, 1tr, 1htr, 1dc) into ring, rep from * 3 or 4 times to give 4 or 5 petals, join with a ss into first ch.

Hanging chain: 3ch, slip down 1st bead, 4ch, slip down 2nd bead, 3ch, slip down 3rd bead, 5ch and so on until all beads are in place and chain is required length.

Making up

Pin Irish crochet and Fluffy flowers in place along ends of scarf on RS. Sew in place using matching yarn. Sew spirals and hanging flowers to the edges, dividing them between two ends. Sew a bead in centre of each flower.

Cut each ribbon into 4 sections of similar, but not equal, length. To attach to scarf, fold in half and use crochet hook to draw looped end through a space. Pass cut ends through loop and pull up tight. Fill in any gaps with woollen fringes (use 3 x 40cm/16in lengths together for each fringe). Trim as necessary so that all fringes are approximately same length. Some beads can also be sewn around ends of scarf between flowers.

from beg, ending with a RS row.

Next 4 rows: As 7th–10th rows.

Next 4 rows: As 3rd row.

Last 2 rows: As 7th and 8th rows. Fasten off.

EMBELLISHMENTS:

Note: Use mainly double knitting for spirals. Each flower should be worked in a different colour or colour combination of either yarn.

Spirals: (make 8)

With 5.00mm (UK 6) hook, make 23ch.

1st row: 3tr into 4th ch from hook, 3tr into each ch to end. Fasten off, leaving a 20cm- (8in-) end.

Thread a few beads – between one and three – on to

Nautical sweater

Ahoy there! You'll stand out from the crowd on the beach in this shipshape sweater.

Worked in red, white and blue yarn, this sweater has a distinct nautical influence with stripes on the body and sleeves and button-details on the raglan sleeves.

GETTING STARTED

★★ *Easy treble fabric but plenty of details in design require attention.*

Size:

To fit bust: 81[86:91:97]cm (32[34:36:38]in)

Actual size: 95[100:105:111]cm (37½[39½:41¼:43¾]in)

Length: 53[55:57:59]cm (21[21½:22½:23¼]in)

Sleeve seam: 43[45:47:49]cm (17[17¾:18½:19¼]in)

Note: Figures in square brackets [ ] refer to larger sizes; only one set of figures applies to all sizes

How much yarn:

2[2:3:3] x 50g (1¾oz) balls of Debbie Bliss Rialto DK in colour A – Red (shade 12)

5[6:6:7] balls in colour B – Navy (shade 17)

5[6:6:6] balls in colour C – White (shade 01)

Hooks:

3.50mm (UK 9) crochet hook

4.00mm (UK 8) crochet hook

Additional items:

6 buttons, 2cm (¾in) in diameter

Tension:

17 sts and 10 rows measure 10cm (4in) square over tr on 4.00mm (UK 8) hook

IT IS ESSENTIAL TO WORK TO THE STATED TENSION TO ACHIEVE SUCCESS

What you have to do:

Work lower hems, cuffs and neckband in relief trebles to form rib pattern. Work main fabric in trebles and stripes as directed. Shape raglan armholes, neckline and sleeves as directed. Work button borders onto front raglan shaping in double crochet.

The Yarn

Debbie Bliss Rialto DK (approx. 105m/114 yards per 50g/1¾oz ball) contains 100% merino wool. It produces a luxurious fabric with good stitch definition that can be machine washed at a low temperature. As well as red, white and blue, there is a wide choice of other colours.

 ## Instructions

Note: When changing colour, always complete last part of last st in old colour with new colour.

BACK:

With 3.50mm (UK 9) hook and A, make 83[87:91:97]ch.

Foundation row: (RS) 1tr into 4th ch from hook, 1tr into each ch to end, turn. 81[85:89:95] sts.

1st row: 3ch (counts as first tr), miss st at base of ch, 1rtrb, *1rtrf, 1rtrb, rep from * to end, 1tr into 3rd of 3ch, turn.

2nd row: 3ch, miss st at base of ch, 1rtrf, *1rtrb, 1rtrf, rep from * to end, 1tr into 3rd of 3ch, turn.

Rep last 2 rows once more to form rib patt, then work 1st row again, changing to B at end of last row.

Change 4.00mm (UK 8) hook.

1st row: (RS) With B, 3ch (counts as first tr), miss st at base of ch, 1tr into each st to end, working last tr in 3rd of 3ch, turn.

Abbreviations:

beg = beginning
ch = chain
cm = centimetre(s)
cont = continue
dc = double crochet
dec = decreased
inc = increas(es)(ed)(ing)
patt = pattern
rem = remain
rep = repeat
RS = right side
rtrb = relief tr back: inserting hook from right to left and from back to front, work 1 tr around stem of next st
rtrf = relief tr front: inserting hook from right to left and from front to back, work 1 tr around stem of next st
ss = slip stitch
st(s) = stitch(es)
tr = treble
WS = wrong side

Rep last row 5 times more. Cont in tr, work 2 rows C, 4 rows B and 2 rows C. Change to B. Cont straight until work measures 32cm (12½in) from beg, ending with a WS row.

Shape raglan armholes:

Next row: Ss into each of first 6 sts, 3ch, miss st at base of ch, 1tr into each tr to last 5 sts, turn.
Rep last row once more.
61[65:69:75] sts.
Next row: 3ch, miss first 2 sts, 1tr into each tr to last 2 sts, miss next tr, 1tr into 3rd of 3ch, turn. 1 st dec at each end of row. ** Rep last row until 29[29:29:31] sts rem. Fasten off.

FRONT:

Work as given for Back to **.
Rep last row until 37[37:37:39] sts rem.

Shape neck:

1st row: 3ch, miss first 2 sts, 1tr into each of next 10tr, turn.
2nd row: Ss into each of first 5 sts, 3ch, miss st at base of ch, 1tr into each of next 4tr, miss last tr, 1tr into 3rd of 3ch, turn.
3rd row: 3ch, miss first 2 sts, 1tr into each of next 2tr, miss last tr, 1tr into 3rd of 3ch, turn.

4th row: 3ch, miss first st, 1tr into next tr, miss last tr, 1tr into 3rd of 3ch. Fasten off.
Return to sts at base of neck, miss centre 13[13:13:15] sts, rejoin yarn to next st, 3ch, miss st at base of ch, 1tr into each of next 9tr, miss last tr, 1tr into 3rd of 3ch, turn.
Next row: 3ch, miss first 2 sts, 1tr into each of next 5tr, turn.
Next row: 3ch, miss first 2 sts, 1tr into each of next 2tr, miss last tr, 1tr into 3rd of 3ch, turn.
Next row: 3ch, miss first 2 sts, 1tr into next tr, 1tr into 3rd of 3ch. Fasten off.

SLEEVES: (make 2)

With 3.50mm (UK 9) hook and A, make 43[45:47:51]ch. Work foundation row as given for Back. 41[43:45:49] sts. Work 5 rows in rib patt as given for Back, changing to C at end of last row.
Change to 4.00mm (UK 8) hook.
Inc row: (RS) With C, 3ch, miss st at base of ch, 1tr into each of next 4[5:6:8] tr, (2tr into next tr, 1tr into each of next 4tr) 6 times, 2tr into next tr, 1tr into each of last 4[5:6:8]tr, 1tr into 3rd of 3ch, turn. 48[50:52:56] sts.

1st–3rd rows: Work straight in tr.

4th row: 3ch, 1tr into st at base of ch, 1tr into each st to end, 2tr into 3rd of 3ch, turn. 1 st inc at each end of row. Inc 1 st at each end of every 4th row, work a further 13[13:15:17] rows. 56[58:60:66] sts. Cont in stripe patt of 2 rows B, 4 rows C and 2 rows B, AT SAME TIME inc 1 st at each end of 2nd[2nd:1st:2nd] row and every foll 3rd row. Using C only, cont to inc at each end of every 3rd row until there are 66[70:74:80] sts. Cont straight until Sleeve measures 43[45:47:49]cm (17[17¾:18½:19¼]in) from beg, ending with a WS row.

Shape raglan sleeve top:

Next row: Ss into each of first 6 sts, 3ch, miss st at base of ch, 1tr into each tr to last 5 sts, turn. Rep last row once more. 46[50:54:60] sts.

Next 3 rows: 3ch, miss first 2 sts, 1tr into each tr to last 2 sts, miss next tr, 1tr into 3rd of 3ch, turn. 1 st dec at each end of row.

Next row: Work straight in tr.

Rep last 4 rows twice more. 28[32:36:42] sts. Now dec 1 st at each end of every row as before until 24[24:24:26] sts rem.

Shape neck:

Next row: 3ch, miss first 2 sts, 1tr into each of next 6tr, turn.

Next row: Ss into each of first 4 sts, 3ch, miss st at base of ch, 1tr into next st, miss 1tr, 1tr into 3rd of 3ch. Fasten off. With RS facing, return to sts on sleeve, miss centre 8[8:8:10] sts and rejoin yarn to next st, 3ch, miss st at base of ch, 1tr into each of next 5tr, miss last tr, 1tr into 3rd of 3ch, turn.

Next row: 3ch, miss first 2 sts, 1tr into each of next 2tr. Fasten off.

FRONT NECKBAND:

With 3.50mm (UK 9) hook and RS of work facing, join A to top of left front neck slope, 3ch, work 11tr down left side of neck, 1tr into each of centre 13[13:13:15] sts and 12tr up right side of neck. 37[37:37:39] sts. Work 2 rows in rib patt as given for Back. Fasten off.

BACK AND SLEEVE NECKBAND:

Sew raglan shaping on Sleeves to raglan shaping on Back. With 3.50mm (UK 9) hook and RS of work facing, join A to top of right front sleeve shaping, 3ch, work 7tr down first slope of right sleeve shaping, 1tr into each of centre 8[8:8:10] sts, work 8tr up second slope of sleeve shaping, 1tr into each of 29[29:29:31] sts at back neck, work 8tr

down slope of left sleeve shaping, 1tr into each of centre 8[8:8:10] sts and 8tr up second slope of sleeve shaping. 77[77:77:83] sts. Work 2 rows in rib patt as given for Back. Fasten off.

FRONT BUTTON BORDERS:

With 3.50mm (UK 9) hook and RS of work facing, join A to top of right front neckband, 1ch (does not count as a st), work 38[42:46:50]dc evenly along raglan shaping, omitting 10 sts at underarm, turn.

Next row: 1ch, 1dc into each dc to end, turn. Rep last row 5 times more. Fasten off. Work left front raglan to match.

Making up

Join 10 sts at underarms on front and sleeve raglans. Sew raglan edge of sleeves to WS of front along first row of dc. Placing front button borders over sleeves, secure lower end and top end. Sew 3 buttons, evenly spaced, on to front button borders. Join side and sleeve seams, matching contrast ribs and stripes.

Colour-block throw

Bright bold colours are used to great effect in this simple yet dramatic throw.

These large square motifs worked in aran yarn and a fabulous array of contrasting colours, each bordered in cream, make a great visual impact when sewn together into a throw.

GETTING STARTED

Squares are easy to work, but care is needed with assembly and border for a professional finish.

Size:
Finished throw measures 154 x 104cm (60 x 41in)

How much yarn:
Debbie Bliss Rialto Aran
5 x 50g (1¾oz) balls in each of colours A – Light Green (shade 10) and B – Light Blue (shade 23)
4 balls in each of colours C – Fuchsia (shade 27); D – Dark Blue (shade 11); E – Red (shade 18) and F – Cream (shade 16)
1 ball in colour G – Dark Green (shade 09)

Hook:
5.00mm (UK 6) crochet hook

Tension:
First 4 rounds measure 10cm (4in) square and completed square measures 25cm (10in) square on 5.00mm (UK 6) hook
IT IS ESSENTIAL TO WORK TO THE STATED TENSION TO ACHIEVE SUCCESS

What you have to do:
Make a square motif in main colour and rounds of trebles with chain spaces at corners. Work final round in contrast colour and double crochet. Make 24 squares in total in six different colours. Sew squares together, then work border in contrast colour.

The Yarn
Debbie Bliss Rialto Aran (approx. 80m/87 yards per 50g/1¾oz ball) contains 100% extra fine merino wool. It produces a soft, luxurious fabric, yet is easy to look after. There is a fantastic range of shades suitable for colour work.

Instructions

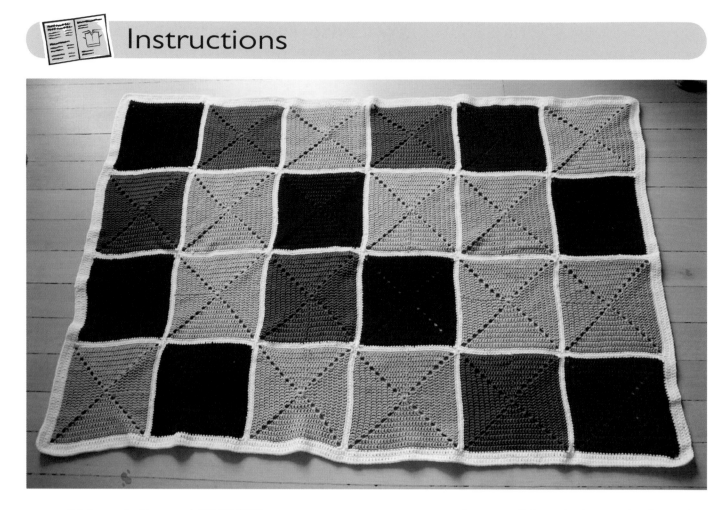

Abbreviations:

ch = chain
cm = centimetre(s)
dc = double crochet
rep = repeat
RS = right side
sp = space
ss = slip stitch
st(s) = stitch(es)
tr = treble

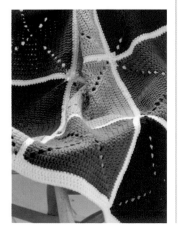

THROW:
Square:

With 5.00mm (UK 6) hook and main colour (A, B, C, D, E or G), make 5ch, join with a ss into first ch to form a ring.

1st round: 3ch (counts as first tr), 2tr into ring, 2ch, *3tr into ring, 2ch, rep from * twice more, join with a ss into 3rd of 3ch.

2nd round: 3ch, miss st at base of ch, 1tr into each of next 2tr, *(1tr, 3ch and 1tr) into next 2ch sp, 1tr into each of next 3tr, rep from * twice more, (1tr, 3ch and 1tr) into next 2ch sp, join with a ss into 3rd of 3ch.

3rd round: 3ch, miss st at base of ch, 1tr into each of next 3tr, *(2tr, 3ch and 2tr) into next 3ch sp, 1tr into each of next 5tr, rep from * twice more, (2tr, 3ch and 2tr) into next 3ch sp, 1tr into next tr, join with a ss into 3rd of 3ch.

4th round: 3ch, miss st at base of ch, 1tr into each of next 5tr, *(2tr, 3ch and 2tr) into next 3ch sp, 1tr into each of next 9tr, rep from * twice more, (2tr, 3ch and 2tr) into next 3ch sp, 1tr into each of next 3tr, join with a ss into 3rd of 3ch.

5th round: 3ch, miss st at base of ch, 1tr into each of next 7tr, *(2tr, 3ch and 2tr) into next 3ch sp, 1tr into each of next 13tr, rep from * twice more, (2tr, 3ch and 2tr) into next 3ch sp, 1tr into each of next 5tr, join with a ss into 3rd of 3ch.

6th round: 3ch, miss st at base of ch, 1tr into each of next 9tr, *(2tr, 3ch and 2tr) into next 3ch sp, 1tr into each of next 17tr, rep from * twice more, (2tr, 3ch and 2tr) into next 3ch sp, 1tr into each of next 7tr, join with a ss into 3rd of 3ch.

7th round: 3ch, miss st at base of ch, 1tr into each of next 11tr, *(2tr, 3ch and 2tr) into next 3ch sp, 1tr into each of next 21tr, rep from * twice more, (2tr, 3ch and 2tr) into next 3ch sp, 1tr into each of next 9tr, join with a ss into 3rd of 3ch.

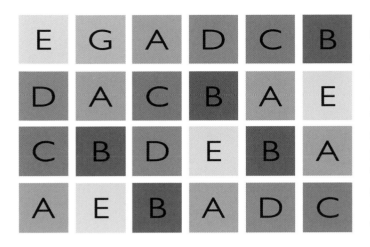

E	G	A	D	C	B
D	A	C	B	A	E
C	B	D	E	B	A
A	E	B	A	D	C

8th round: 3ch, miss st at base of ch, 1tr into each of next 13tr, *(2tr, 3ch and 2tr) into next 3ch sp, 1tr into each of next 25tr, rep from * twice more, (2tr, 3ch and 2tr) into next 3ch sp, 1tr into each of next 11tr, join with a ss into 3rd of 3ch.

9th round: 3ch, miss st at base of ch, 1tr into each of next 15tr, *(2tr, 3ch and 2tr) into next 3ch sp, 1tr into each of next 29tr, rep from * twice more, (2tr, 3ch and 2tr) into next 3ch sp, 1tr into each of next 13tr, join with a ss into 3rd of 3ch. Fasten off.

10th round: Join F to any 3ch sp, 1ch (does not count as a st), *5dc into 3ch sp, 1dc into each of next 33tr, rep from * 3 times more, join with a ss into first dc. Fasten off, leaving a 50cm (20in) length of yarn for sewing squares together.

Make 24 squares in total in the following colours, always using F for the last round:

6 in A, 5 in B, 4 in C, 4 in D, 4 in E and 1 in G.

Making up

Lay the squares out, RS up, in four rows of six, arranging colours as shown in diagram. Starting at top row, sew the first square to next along side edges, sliding needle under two loops at top of each dc on both squares. Add next four squares in the same way, then make up other three rows in same way. Finally, sew four rows together as before.

Border:

With 5.00mm (UK 6) hook and RS facing, join F to first of 5dc at one corner, 3ch, 1tr into next dc, *3tr into next dc (centre of 5dc), 1tr into each dc to centre of 5dc at next corner, rep from * twice more, 3tr into next dc, 1tr into each dc to end, join with a ss into 3rd of 3ch.

Next round: 3ch, miss st at base of ch, 1tr into each of next 2tr, *3tr into next tr (centre of 3tr), 1tr into each tr to centre of 3tr at next corner, rep from * twice more, 3tr into next tr, 1tr into each tr to end, join with a ss into 3rd of 3ch. Fasten off.

Stetson-style hat

Shade yourself from the sun with this fun hat, which has a touch of the wild West.

Worked in double crochet and two strands of yarn together, this hat with a flexible brim has a 'ribbon band' worked into the fabric.

The Yarn

Rowan Savannah (approx. 80m/ 87 yards per 50g/1¾oz ball) is an aran-weight yarn containing 94% cotton and 6% silk. The matt cotton fibres are bound together with an extremely fine shiny silk thread to create a very distinctive yarn. There is a small range of chalky desert shades.

GETTING STARTED

★★★ *Working with two strands of yarn together requires some effort to make a firm fabric.*

Size:
To fit an average-sized woman's head

How much yarn:
4 x 50g (1¾oz) balls of Rowan Savannah in colour A – Bare (shade 931)
1 ball in each of colour B – Arid (shade 933) and colour C – Barren (shade 937)

Hook:
5.50mm (UK 5) crochet hook

Additional items:
2m (2¼ yards) of 1mm- (¹⁄₁₆in-) thick flexible garden wire

Tension:
13 sts and 14 rows measure 10cm (4in) square over dc with two strands of yarn on 5.50mm (UK 5) hook
IT IS ESSENTIAL TO WORK TO THE STATED TENSION TO ACHIEVE SUCCESS

What you have to do:
Work throughout in rounds of double crochet, joining each round or working in a continuous spiral as directed. Start in centre of top of crown by working around both sides of foundation chain. Shape pointed front of crown, rounded back of crown and brim by increasing. Work last round of brim over flexible wire.

Instructions

Abbreviations:

beg = beginning
ch = chain(s)
cm = centimetre(s)
dc = double crochet
foll = follows
RS = right side
sp = space
ss = slip stitch
st(s) = stitch(es)

Note:

Work throughout using two strands of yarn together.

HAT:
Top of crown:

With 5.50mm (UK 5) hook and two strands of A, make 8ch.

1st round: (RS) 1dc in 4th ch from hook, 1dc in each of next 3ch, 3dc in last ch, then work in opposite side of foundation ch as foll: 1dc in each of next 4ch, 4dc in next 3ch sp, join with a ss in first dc. 15dc.

2nd round: 1ch (counts as first dc), 1dc in each of next 3dc, 2dc in next dc, (1dc, 2ch, 1dc) in next dc (front of hat), 2dc in next dc, 1dc in each of next 4dc, 2dc in each of next 4dc (back of hat), join with a ss in first ch. 22dc.

3rd round: 1ch, miss st at base of ch, 1dc in each of next 4dc, 2dc in next dc, 1dc in next dc, (1dc, 2ch, 1dc) in next 2ch sp, 1dc in next dc, 2dc in next dc, 1dc in each of next 5dc, (2dc in next dc, 1dc in next dc) 4 times, join with a ss in first ch. 30dc.

4th round: 1ch, miss st at base of ch, 1dc in each of next 6dc, 2dc in next dc, 1dc in next dc, (1dc, 2ch, 1dc) in next 2ch sp, 1dc in next dc, 2dc in next dc, 1dc in each of next 7dc, (2dc in next dc, 1dc in each of next 2dc) 4 times, join with a ss in first ch. 38dc.

5th round: 1ch, miss st at base of ch, 1dc in each of next 8dc, 2dc in next dc, 1dc in next dc, (1dc, 2ch, 1dc) in next 2ch sp, 1dc in next dc, 2dc in next dc, 1dc in each of next 9dc, (2dc in next dc, 1dc in each of next 3dc) 4 times, join with a ss in first ch. 46dc.

6th round: 1ch, miss st at base of ch, 1dc in each of next 12dc, (1dc, 2ch, 1dc) in next 2ch sp, 1dc in each of next 13dc, (2dc in next dc, 1dc in each of next 4dc) 4 times, join with a ss in first ch. 52dc.

7th round: 1ch, miss st at base of ch, 1dc in each of next 13dc, (1dc, 2ch, 1dc) in next 2ch sp, 1dc in each of next 14dc, (2dc in next dc, 1dc in each of next 5dc) 4 times, join with a ss in first ch. 58dc. Insert a marker in first st of each of last 4 increases and move markers up as necessary.

Sides of crown:

8th round: 1ch, miss st at base of ch, 1dc in back loop only of each dc and ch all round, join with a ss in first ch. 60dc.

Working into both loops of sts, marking beg of round and moving markers as necessary, work in continuous rounds (without joining) as foll:

9th round: 1ch, miss st at base of ch, 1dc in each dc all round, working 2dc in each marked st. 64dc.

10th round: Work in dc.

11th round: As 9th. 68dc.

12th round: As 10th.

13th round: As 9th. 72dc.

14th–16th rounds: As 10th.

17th round: As 9th. 76dc.

18th round: As 10th, but join with a ss in first ch. Fasten off A.

19th round: Join in B to same place as ss, 1ch, miss st at base of ch, 1dc in each dc all round, join with a ss in first ch. Fasten off B.

20th–22nd rounds: Join in C to same place as ss and work as 19th round. Fasten off C.

23rd round: As 19th.

Brim:

Join in A. Marking beg of rounds and moving marker as necessary, work in continuous rounds of A as foll:

24th round: 1ch, miss st at base of ch, working in front loop only of sts, 1dc in next 9dc, 2dc in next dc, (1dc in each of next 12dc, 2dc in next dc) 5 times. 82dc.

25th round: As 10th.

26th round: 1dc in each of first 6dc, 2dc in next dc, (1dc in each of next 7dc, 2dc in next dc, 1dc in each of next 6dc, 2dc in next dc) 5 times. 93 sts.

27th round: As 10th.

28th round: (2dc in next dc, 1dc in each of next 4dc) 17 times, 2dc in next dc, 1dc in each of last 7dc. 111dc.

29th round: As 10th.

30th round: (2dc in next dc, 1dc in each of next 9dc) 11 times, 1dc in last dc. 122dc.

31st round: As 10th, but join with a ss in first dc.

32nd round: Working over wire folded double, 1ch, miss st at base of ch, 1dc into each st all round, join with a ss into first ch. Fasten off.

Poncho coat

This poncho is so comfortable that you'll find it hard to leave behind when the days turn warmer.

Worked in a soft fabric and with a knitted ribbed collar, this poncho has buttons sewn on either side of its distinctive centre front to suggest the styling of a double-breasted coat.

The Yarn

Sirdar Eco Wool DK (approx. 100m/120 yards per 50g/1¾oz ball) contains 100% wool in a double knitting weight. Loosely spun, it results in a soft, dense hand-wash fabric. It comes in natural shades.

GETTING STARTED

★ ★ *Simple pattern to keep correct and increasing is easy to follow once it is established.*

Size:
To suit bust: 81[86:91:97]cm (32[34:36:38]in)
Length: 70[70:72:72]cm (27½[27½:28¼:28¼]in) at centre point
Note: *Figures in square brackets [ ] refer to larger sizes; where there is only one set of figures, it applies to all sizes*

How much yarn:
12[13:15:16] x 50g (1¾oz) balls of Sirdar Eco Wool in Natural (shade 201)

Hook:
5.00mm (UK 6) crochet hook

Additional items:
4.00mm (UK 8) and 5.00mm (UK 6) circular knitting needles (maximum length 40cm/16in) for collar
4 x 28mm (1⅛ in) buttons

Tension:
8 Vs measure 12cm (4¾in) and 10 rows measure 10cm (4in) on 5.00mm (UK 6) hook
IT IS ESSENTIAL TO WORK TO THE STATED TENSION TO ACHIEVE SUCCESS

What you have to do:
Make poncho in rounds, working throughout in V pattern. Increase at either side of centre front and back. Work crab stitch edging along lower edge. Pick up stitches around neckline and knit collar in rounds of double rib.

Instructions

BACK AND FRONT:

(made in one piece)
With 5.00mm (UK 6) hook make 87[95:103:111]ch for neck edge.

Foundation round: 1 tr into 4th ch from hook, *miss next ch, 2tr into next ch to form a V, rep from * to last ch, miss last ch, join with a ss into 3rd of 3ch to form a circle. 42[46:50:54] Vs. Do not turn but cont in rounds as foll:

Inc round: 3ch (counts as first tr), 1 tr into sp at centre of first V (this is centre back), 2tr between first and second V to inc 1 V, work 1 V into sp at centre of next 20[22:24:26] Vs, 1 V between previous V and next V to inc 1 V, work 1 V into next V and mark this V (this is centre front), 1 V between previous V and next

V to inc 1 V, work 1 V into each of next 20[22:24:26] Vs, 1 V between previous V and first V to inc 1 V, join with a ss into 3rd of 3ch. 4 Vs inc.

Cont in V patt, moving marker up on every round and working increases at each side of V at centre back and front as foll:

Next round: 3ch, 1 tr into first V, 1 V into each V all round, join with a ss into 3rd of 3ch.

Inc round: 3ch, 1 tr into first V, inc 1 V between Vs, patt to marked V, inc 1 V between Vs, 1 V into marked V, inc 1 V between Vs, patt to end, inc 1 V between Vs, join with a ss into 3rd of 3ch. 4 Vs inc. The last 2 rows form patt. Cont in patt until there are 76[78:82:84] Vs between centre front and centre back Vs on each side.

Next round: Working from left to right instead of from right to left, work 1 dc into each tr (crab st), join with a ss into first dc. Fasten off.

COLLAR:

With 4.00mm (UK 8) circular knitting needle, RS facing and working in rem loop on foundation ch, pick up and k88[92:96:104] sts around neck edge. Place a marker at beg of round and cont in rounds of rib as foll:

Next round: (P2, k2) to end.

Rep last round for 4cm (1½in).

Change to 5.00mm (UK 6) circular knitting needle.

Inc round: *P1, pup, p1, k1, puk, k1, rep from * to end. 132[138:144:156] sts.

Next round: (P3, k3) to end. Rep last round until collar measures 11cm (4¼in) from beg. Cast off knitwise.

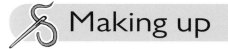

Making up

Press lightly on wrong side using a warm iron over a damp cloth and omitting collar. Mark two pairs of button positions on front, the first pair 9cm (3½in) from centre of neck edge and 4cm (1½in) either side of centre V, and the second pair 10cm (4in) below. Sew on buttons at marked positions.

HOW TO
WORK THE V PATTERN

This easy pattern creates a lovely texture and once you have identified where to place the pairs of stitches it is quick to work. For the poncho the pattern is worked in the round.

1 Make the foundation chain as instructed and then begin the pattern by working one treble into the fourth chain from the hook. Miss one chain and work two trebles into the next chain. This forms one V-stitch. Repeat this to the end of the chain and then follow the instructions to form the work into a circle.

2 Make a turning chain of three chains (this counts as the first treble), one treble into first space and continue the pattern by working a pair of trebles into the space between the pair of trebles forming one V-stich in the previous row. Instructions are also given for increasing the number of stitches by working pairs of trebles in between the V-stitches of the previous row.

3 The pattern works up quickly and will look like this with each pair of trebles placed in the V formed by the pairs of trebles (V-stitches) in the previous row.

Mini rag-rug placemats

Create a Mediterranean alfresco feel with these mats.

These colourful and practical mats are worked in rows of trebles from strips of fabric. The ends are trimmed with fringes made from string.

GETTING STARTED

⭐⭐ *Easy stitches but working with strips of fabric requires practice.*

Size:

Mat measures approximately 35 x 30cm (14 x 12in), excluding fringing

How much yarn:

Selection of dress-weight cotton fabrics, cut into continuous 2–2.5cm (¾–1in) wide strips (as a guide, each row uses almost 4m (4½ yards) of fabric strip and each mat consists of 13 rows)

Hooks:

6.00mm (UK 4) crochet hook
10.00mm (UK 000) crochet hook

Additional item:

Ball of string or unbleached craft cotton

Tension:

6 sts measure 10cm (4in) and 3 rows measure 8cm (3⅛in) over tr on 10.00mm (UK 000) hook

What you have to do:

Cut up fabrics as directed. Work throughout in trebles. Knot string fringe along each end.

The Yarn

This design is based on a rag-rug technique and uses strips of fabric instead of yarn. The fabrics can be any old cotton dress-weight material (plain and patterned) and they should be washed first. Afterwards the fabrics should be cut in strips as described on pages 86–87.

Instructions

Note:
You can prepare the fabric first and roll it up into small balls, or cut each piece as you go. Cut a strip approximately 2–2.5cm (¾–1in) wide from one edge of the piece of fabric and stop cutting when you are about 2–2.5cm (¾–1in) from the far end. Now turn the fabric and start cutting a further 2–2.5cm (¾–1in) down, so that you have one long strip. Continue in this way until the end of the piece of fabric.

MAT:

With 10.00mm (UK 000) hook and first colour, make 20ch.

Foundation row: (WS) 1tr into 4th ch from hook, 1tr into each ch to end, turn. 18 sts.

Patt row: 3ch (counts as first tr), miss st at base of ch, 1tr into each st to end, working last tr into 3rd of 3ch, turn. Rep last row 11 times more, changing colour after each row, or after two rows for wider stripes. When changing colour, always work last part of last st in new colour before turning. Fasten off.

Fringe:

Cut two or three 15cm (6in) strands of string or craft cotton for each tassel. Fold strands in half and, using 6.00mm (UK 4) hook, pull folded ends through top of first tr in last row worked. Remove hook and draw loose ends through loop; pull up tightly. Repeat to knot a tassel into each tr along same edge and into single strands of foundation ch along opposite end.

Trim fringe evenly.

HOW TO
CUT THE FABRIC

Old cotton fabric, either plain or patterned, is perfect for this technique.
Cut it into strips, roll into balls, and you're ready to start crocheting these funky mats.

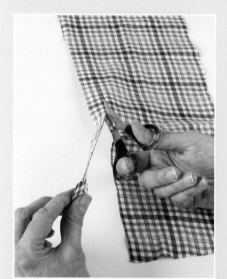

1 Select a mixture of cotton fabrics with a similar colour palette. They can be patterned, striped, checked or plain. Wash the fabric first and then cut it into strips approximately 2–2.5cm (¾–1in) wide.

2 To make a continuous strip, stop cutting when you are 2–2.5cm (¾–1in) from the end of the piece and turn the fabric. Continue cutting in the opposite direction; repeat this each time you reach the edge of the fabric.

3 This will give you a long continuous strip of fabric that is 2–2.5cm (¾–1in) wide. Wind each strip up into a small ball. Repeat this with each fabric. You are then ready to work.

Change colours as you wish, swapping from ball to ball.

Loop-neck sweater

This pretty top is soft, cosy and incredibly light to wear.

This classic fitted sweater with a softly draping looped neckline is worked in a beautiful comfortably soft alpaca yarn.

GETTING STARTED

⭐⭐ *Straightforward pattern with easy stitches, but work must be kept neat for a professional finish.*

Size:
To fit bust: *81[86:91:97]cm (32[34:36:38]in)*
Actual size: *91[97:102:107]cm (36[38:40:42]in)*
Length: *59[61:64:66]cm (23¼[24:25¼:26]in)*
Sleeve seam: *45cm (17¾in)*
Note: *Figures in square brackets [ ] refer to larger sizes; where there is only one set of figures, it applies to all sizes*

How much yarn:
9[9:10:10] x 50g (1¾oz) balls of Artesano 4-ply Alpaca in Sweet Pea (shade CA13)

Hooks:
3.50mm (UK 9) crochet hook
4.00mm (UK 8) crochet hook

Tension:
19 sts and 16 rows measure 10cm (4in) square over patt on 3.50mm (UK 9) hook
IT IS ESSENTIAL TO WORK TO THE STATED TENSION TO ACHIEVE SUCCESS

What you have to do:
Work throughout in pattern of alternating rows of double crochet and trebles. Shape armholes, neckline, sleeves and collar as directed.

The Yarn
Artesano 4-ply Alpaca (approx. 184m/201 yards per 50g/1¾oz ball) contains 100% superfine alpaca. This yarn produces a luxurious fabric that is a delight both to touch and to wear. There is a large range of colours.

 # Instructions

BACK:
With 4.00mm (UK 8) hook make 99[104:109:114]ch.
Change to 3.50mm (UK 9) hook.
Foundation row: (RS) 1tr in 4th ch from hook, 1tr in each ch to end, turn. 97[102:107:112] sts.
Cont in patt as foll:
1st row: 1ch (counts as first dc), miss st at base of ch, 1dc in each st to end, working last dc in top of turning ch, turn.
2nd row: 2ch (counts as first tr), miss st at base of ch, 1tr in each st to end, working last st in 1ch, turn.
These 2 rows form patt. Work 7 more rows in patt, ending with a WS row.

Next row: (RS) 2ch, miss st at base of ch, 1tr in each of next 30[31:32:33] sts, tr2tog over next 2 sts, 1tr in each of next 31[34:37:40] sts, tr2tog over next 2 sts, 1tr in each of next 31[32:33:34] sts, turn. 95[100:105:110] sts.
Work 9 rows straight.
Next row: (RS) 2ch, miss st at base of ch, 1tr in each of next 29[30:31:32] sts, tr2tog over next 2 sts, 1tr in each of next 31[34:37:40] sts, tr2tog over next 2 sts, 1tr in each of next 30[31:32:33] sts, turn. 93[98:103:108] sts.
Cont to dec in this way, working one st less at each end, on every foll 10th row 3 times more. 87[92:97:102] sts.

Abbreviations:

alt = alternate
ch = chain(s)
cm = centimetre(s)
cont = continue
dc = double crochet
dec = decrease
dtr = double treble
foll = follow(s)(ing)
inc = increase(d)
patt = pattern
rep = repeat
RS = right side
ss = slip stitch
st(s) = stitch(es)
tog = together
tr = treble
tr2(3)tog = (yrh, insert hook into next st and draw a loop through, yrh and draw through first 2 loops on hook) 2(3) times, yrh and draw through all 3(4) loops on hook
WS = wrong side
yrh = yarn round hook

Patt 11[13:15:17] rows straight, ending with a WS row.

Shape armholes:

1st row: (RS) 1ch, miss st at base of ch, ss into each of next 6[7:7:8] sts, 3ch, miss st at base of ch, tr3tog over next 3 sts, 1tr in each st to last 10[11:11:12] sts, tr3tog over next 3 sts, 1dtr in next st, turn. 71[74:79:82] sts.

2nd row: 1ch, miss st at base of ch, 1dc in each st to end, working last dc in top of 3ch, turn.

3rd row: 3ch, miss st at base of ch, tr3tog over next 3 sts, 1tr in each st to last 4 sts, tr3tog over next 3 sts, 1dtr in 1ch, turn. Rep 2nd and 3rd rows 2[2:3:3] times more. 59[62:63:66] sts.**

Work 21[23:23:25] rows straight, ending with a WS row.

Shape neck:

1st row: (RS) 2ch, miss st at base of ch, 1tr in each of next 15[16:16:17] sts, tr3tog over next 3 sts, 1dtr in next st, turn. 18[19:19:20] sts.

2nd row: 1ch, miss st at base of ch, 1dc in each st to end, turn.

3rd row: 2ch, miss st at base of ch, 1tr in each of next 13[14:14:15] sts, tr3tog over

next 3 sts, 1dtr in 1ch, turn. 16[17:17:18] sts.

4th row: As 2nd row. Fasten off.

Next row: (RS) Miss centre 19[20:21:22] sts, rejoin yarn to next st, 3ch, miss st at base of ch, tr3tog over next 3 sts, 1tr in each st to end, turn. 18[19:19:20] sts.

Next row: 1ch, miss st at base of ch, 1dc in each st to end, turn.

Next row: 3ch, miss st at base of ch, tr3tog over next 3 sts, 1tr in each st to end, turn. 16[17:17:18] sts.

Next row: 1ch, miss st at base of ch, 1dc in each st to end. Fasten off.

FRONT:

Work as given for Back to **.
Work 11[13:13:15] rows straight, ending with a WS row.

Shape neck:

1st row: (RS) 2ch, miss st at base of ch, 1tr in each of next 17[18:18:19] sts, tr3tog over next 3 sts, 1dtr in next st, turn. 20[21:21:22] sts.

2nd row: 1ch, miss st at base of ch, 1dc in each st to end, turn.

3rd row: 2ch, miss st at base of ch, 1tr in each st to last 4 sts, tr3tog over next 3 sts, 1dtr in 1ch, turn.

Rep 2nd and 3rd rows once more. 16[17:17:18] sts. Work 9 rows straight. Fasten off.

Next row: (RS) Miss centre 15[16:17:18] sts, rejoin yarn to next st, 3ch, miss st at base of ch, tr3tog over next 3 sts, 1tr in each st to end, turn.

Complete to match first side of neck.

SLEEVES: (make 2)

With 4.00mm (UK 8) hook make 46[48:50:52]ch. Change to 3.50mm (UK 9) hook. Work foundation row as given for Back. 44[46:48:50] sts.

Cont in patt as given for Back, work 5[1:5:1] rows straight, ending with a WS row.

Next row: (RS) 2ch, miss st at base of ch, 2tr in next st, 1tr in each st to last 2 sts, 2tr in next st, 1tr in 1ch, turn. 1 st inc at each end of row.

Cont to inc in this way at each end of every foll 6th[6th:5th:5th] row 10[11:12:13] times more. 66[70:74:78] sts. Work 5[3:5:4] rows straight, ending with a WS row.

Shape top:

1st row: (RS) As 1st row of Back armhole shaping. 50[52:56:58] sts. Patt 1 row.

3rd row: As 3rd row of Back armhole shaping. Patt 1 row.

5th row: 3ch, miss st at base of ch, tr2tog over next 2 sts, 1tr in each st to last 3 sts, tr2tog over next 2 sts, 1dtr in 1ch, turn. 44[46:50:52] sts.

Cont to dec one st at each end of row in this way on every foll alt row 7 times more. 30[32:36:38] sts. Now dec as given for 3rd row on foll 2[2:3:3] alt rows. 22[24:24:26] sts. Fasten off.

COLLAR:

Join shoulder seams as foll: with RS tog, over-sew single inner strand of each pair of edge sts to form a flat st seam. With 4.00mm (UK 8) hook make 33[33:35:35]ch. Change to 3.50mm (UK 9) hook.

Foundation row: (RS) 2tr in 4th ch from hook, 1tr in each ch to last 3ch, tr2tog over next 2ch, 1tr in last ch, turn. 31[31:33:33] sts.

1st row: 1ch (counts as first dc), miss st at base of ch, 1dc in each st to end, working last dc in 3rd of 3ch, turn.

2nd row: 3ch (counts as first tr), miss st at base of ch, 2tr in next st, 1tr in each st to last 3 sts, tr2tog over next 2 sts, 1tr in 3rd of 3ch, turn.

Rep last 2 rows until collar fits loosely around neck edge. Fasten off.

LOOP:

With 4.00mm (UK 8) hook make 29ch. Change to 3.50mm (UK 9) hook. Work foundation row as given for Back. 27 sts. Cont in patt as given for Back, work 12 rows. Fasten off.

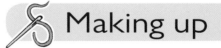

Making up

Press lightly according to directions on ball band. Sew in sleeves, then join side and sleeve seams. Join collar into a ring with a flat st seam. With RS facing, position centre seam of collar to centre front neck and back stitch one edge of collar to neck. Fold collar in half to WS and catch down other edge on inside of neck. Fold loop in half lengthways, seam and press it. Fold loop over collar at centre front neck and catch down one end to collar seam on RS and other end to collar seam on WS.

Fish bath mat

Have some aquatic fun in the bathroom with this fish-themed mat.

Worked in bold, bright colours and two strands of a soft cotton yarn, this mat is crocheted in the round to suggest radiating ripples; then the fish motif is made separately and sewn on.

The Yarn

Sublime Soya Cotton DK (approx. 110m/120 yards per 50g/1¾oz ball) is a blend of 50% soya-sourced viscose and 50% cotton. This fibre combination produces a practical yet soft fabric, which can be machine washed. There is a wide range of contemporary colours.

GETTING STARTED

★★ *Not difficult to make, but it is quite a big project and accuracy is required to achieve a good finish.*

Size:
Finished mat measures approximately 58 x 43cm (23 x 17in)

How much yarn:
6 x 50g (1¾oz) balls of Sublime Soya Cotton DK in colour A – Tangiers (shade 149)
1 ball in colour B – Cruiser (shade 151)
2 balls in colour C – Pumpkin (shade 87)

Hooks:
4.00mm (UK 8) crochet hook
5.00mm (UK 6) crochet hook

Tension:
Mat: 11.5 sts and 10.5 rows measure 10cm (4in) square over htr using yarn double on 5.00mm (UK 6) hook
Fish: 19 sts and 21 rows measure 10cm (4in) square over dc using one strand of yarn on 4.00mm (UK 8) hook
IT IS ESSENTIAL TO WORK TO THE STATED TENSION TO ACHIEVE SUCCESS

What you have to do:
Work bath mat in rounds of half trebles using yarn double. Work wavy edging around mat. Make fish motif with head in double crochet and a patterned body. Make separate fins in double crochet. Position fish on mat and sew in place.

 Instructions

MAT:

Note: Use yarn double throughout. With 5.00mm (UK 6) hook and two strands of A, make 21ch.

Foundation row: 1htr into 3rd ch from hook, 1htr into each ch to end, turn. 20 sts.

1st round: 2ch, 1htr into first htr, 1htr into each of next 18htr, 3htr into top of turning ch, working into ch at base of Foundation row work 3htr into first ch, 1htr into each of next 18htr, 3htr into last ch, 1htr into st at base of 2ch, ss into 2nd of 2ch. 48 sts.

2nd round: 2ch, 1htr into same place as ss, 1htr into each of next 20htr, 3htr into next (centre corner) htr, 1htr into each of next 2htr, 3htr into next (centre corner) htr, 1htr into each of next 20htr, 3htr into next (centre corner) htr, 1htr into each of last 2htr, 1htr into same place as first htr of round, ss into 2nd of 2ch. 56 sts.

3rd round: 2ch, 1htr into same place a ss, *1htr into each htr to centre corner htr, 3htr into centre corner htr, rep from * twice, 1htr into each htr, 1htr into same place as first htr of round, ss into 2nd of 2ch. 64 sts.

Abbreviations:

beg = beginning
ch = chain(s)
cm = centimetre(s)
cont = continue
dc = double crochet
dc2tog = (insert hook into next st and draw a loop through) twice, yrh and draw through all 3 loops
dec = decrease(d)
dtr = double treble
foll = follows
htr = half treble
inc = increase(d)
patt(s) = pattern(s)
rem = remain
rep(s) = repeat(s)
RS = right side
sp = space
ss = slip stitch

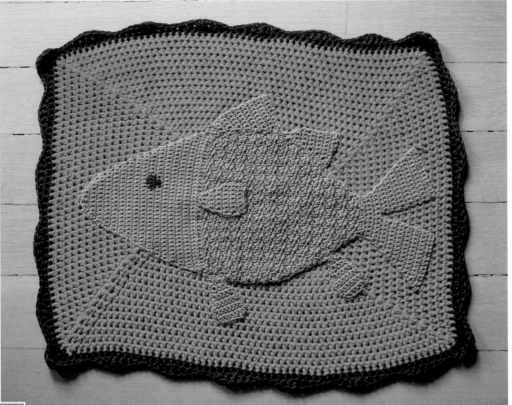

st(s) = stitch(es)
tr = treble
WS = wrong side
yrh = yarn round hook

Rep 3rd round 18 times. 208 sts. Fasten off.

Border:

Join 2 strands of B to same place as ss and work 3rd round.

Next round: 4ch, *1tr into next st, 1htr into next st, 1dc into next st, 1ss into each of next 2 sts, 1dc into next st, 1htr into next st, 1tr into next st, 1dtr into next st **, rep from * to ** 6 times (last dtr is in corner st), work 2 more dtr into corner st, rep from * to ** 5 times (last dtr is in corner st), work 2 more dtr into corner st, rep from * once, ss into 4th of 4ch. Fasten off.

FISH:

Note: Use yarn single throughout. With 4.00mm (UK 8) hook and C, make 4ch.

Foundation row: (RS) 1dc in 2nd ch from hook, 1dc in each of next 2ch, turn. 3 sts.

1st row: 1ch (does not count as a st),

2dc in first st, 1dc in next st, 2dc in last dc, turn. 5 sts.

2nd row: 1ch, 2dc in first st, 1dc in each of next 3 sts, 2dc in last st, turn. 7 sts.

3rd row: 1ch, 2dc in first st, 1dc in each of next 5 sts, 2dc in last st, turn. 9 sts.

4th row: 1ch, 2dc in first st, 1dc in each of next 7 sts, 2dc in last st, turn. 11 sts.

5th row: 1ch, 2dc in first st, 1dc in each of next 9 sts, 2dc in last st, turn. 13 sts.

6th row: 1ch, 1dc in each st to end, turn.

7th row: 1ch, 2dc in first st, 1dc in each st to last st, 2dc in last st, turn. 2 sts inc. Rep last 2 rows until there are 25 sts.

Work eye:

Next row: (RS) 1ch, 1dc in each of next 16 sts, join in B on last part of last st; with B, 1dc in each of next 2 sts, changing back to C on last part of last st; with C, 1dc in each of last 7 sts, turn.

Next row: 1ch, 2dc in first st, 1dc in each of next 5 sts, picking up B on last part of last st; with B, 1dc in each of next 4 sts, changing back to C on last part of last st;

with C, 1dc in each of next 14 sts, 2dc in last st, turn. 27 sts.

Next row: 1ch, 1dc in each of next 16 sts, join in B on last part of last st; with B, 1dc in each of next 4 sts, changing back to C on last part of last st; with C, 1dc in each of last 7 sts, turn.

Next row: 1ch, 2dc in first st, 1dc in each of next 7 sts, picking up B on last part of last st; with B, 1dc in each of next 2 sts, changing back to C on last part of last st; with C, 1dc in each of next 16 sts, 2dc in last st, turn. 29 sts. Now rep 6th and 7th rows until there are 39 sts.

Next row: 1ch, ss in front loop only of each st to end, turn.

Next row: 1ch, working into loops left free 2 rows below, work 2dc in first st, 1dc in each st to last st, 2dc in last st, turn. 41 sts.

Cont in scale patt as foll:

1st row: (RS) 1ch (counts as first dc), miss st at base of ch, *(1dc, 1ch, 1tr) in next st, miss 2 sts, rep from *, ending with 1dc in last st, turn. 13 patts.

2nd row: 1ch, miss st at base of ch, *(1dc, 1ch, 1tr) in next ch sp, rep from *, ending with 1dc in 1ch, turn.

Inc row: 1ch, (1dc, 1ch, 1tr) into first dc, patt to end. 1 patt inc at beg of row.

Rep inc row once more. 15 patts.

Rep 2nd row until work measures 12cm (4¾in) from beg of scale patt, ending with a WS row.

Dec row: (RS) 1ch, miss st at base of ch, ss in ch sp, 1ch, patt to last ch sp, 1dc in ch sp, 1dc in 1ch, turn. 2 sts dec.

Next row: Patt to end, turn. Rep last 2 rows until 10 sts (3 patt reps) rem, ending with a WS row.

Tail:

1st–3rd rows: 1ch (does not count as a st), 1dc in each st to end, turn. 10 sts.

4th row: 1ch, 2dc in first st, 1dc in each st to last st, 2dc in last st, turn. 12 sts.

5th row: 1ch, 2dc in first st, 1dc in each of next 5 sts, turn and cont on these 7 sts.

6th row: 1ch, 1dc in each dc to end, turn.

7th row: 1ch, 2dc in first st, 1dc in each st to end, turn. Rep last 2 rows 5 times more (13 sts), then work 6th row again. Fasten off.

With RS facing, rejoin yarn to next st at base of division, 1ch, 1dc in each of next 5 sts, 2dc in last st, turn.

Complete to match first side of tail, reversing shaping.

Large upper fin:

With 4.00mm (UK 8) hook and C, make 4ch.

Foundation row: 1dc in 2nd ch from hook, 1dc in each of next 2ch, turn. 3 sts.

1st row: (RS) 1ch (does not count as a st), 2dc in first st, 1dc in each st to end, turn. 4 sts.

2nd row: 1ch, 1dc in each st to end, turn.**

Rep last 2 rows until there are 10 sts, ending with a RS row.

Next row: 1ch, 1dc in each of first 5 sts, ss in each of last 5 sts. Fasten off.

Small upper fin:

Work as given for Large upper fin to **.

Rep last 2 rows until there are 8 sts.

Next row: 1ch, 1dc in each of first 4 sts, ss in each of last 4 sts. Fasten off.

Lower fin:

With 4.00mm (UK 8) hook and C, make 4ch.

Foundation row: 1dc in 2nd ch from hook, 1dc in each of next 2ch, turn. 3 sts.

1st row: 1ch (does not count as a st), 1dc in each st to end, turn. ***

2nd row: As 1st row.

3rd row: 1ch, 2dc in first st, 1dc in next st, 2dc in last st, turn. 5 sts.

4th and 5th rows: As 1st and 2nd rows.

6th row: 1ch, 2dc in first st, 1dc in each of next 3 sts, 2dc in last st, turn. 7 sts.

Work 5 more rows in dc.

Next row: 1ch, dc2tog, 1dc in each of next 3 sts, dc2tog. 5 sts. Fasten off.

Body fin:

Work as given for Lower fin to ***. Complete as given for Lower fin from 3rd row.

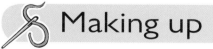

Making up

Place fish motif centrally on bath mat and slip stitch firmly to background fabric all round edge of shape. Sew on fins, using photograph as a guide to positioning.

Colour-block sweater

Make a bold statement with this striking sweater.

This striking sweater in three colours has a relaxed fit with an added section at the top of the yoke forming the top of the sleeves. It is worked in a lightweight 4-ply yarn.

GETTING STARTED

★★ *Requires patience as yarn is quite fine but stitch patterns and shaping are straightforward.*

Size:
To fit bust: *81[86:91:97]cm (32[34:36:38]in)*
Actual size: *92[98:104:108]cm (36¼[38½:41:42½]in)*
Length: *61[61:62:62]cm (24[24:24½:24½]in)*
Sleeve seam: *33cm (13in) plus top of sleeve with yoke*
Note: *Figures in square brackets [ ] refer to larger sizes; where there is only one set of figures, it applies to all sizes*

How much yarn:
5[6:7:8] x 50g (1¾oz) balls of Rowan Cashsoft 4-ply in colour A – Elite (shade 451)
1[4:5:6] balls in colour B – Black (shade 122)
3[3:4:4] balls in colour C – Poppy (shade 438)

Hooks:
3.00mm (UK 11) crochet hook
3.50mm (UK 9) crochet hook

Tension:
10 Vs and 12 rows measure 10cm (4in) square over patt on 3.50mm (UK 9) hook
IT IS ESSENTIAL TO WORK TO THE STATED TENSION TO ACHIEVE SUCCESS

What you have to do:
Work base of back and front in first colour and an easy four-row pattern. Change to second colour for yoke and work in rows of ridged trebles. Shape top of yoke so that it forms top of sleeves. Work sleeves in third colour and pattern, shaping as directed.

The Yarn
Rowan Cashsoft 4-ply (approx. 160m/174 yards per 50g/1¾oz ball) is a blend of 57% extra-fine merino wool, 33% acrylic microfibre and 10% cashmere. It produces a fine fabric with good stitch definition that drapes well. It is machine washable, with a wide colour range.

Instructions

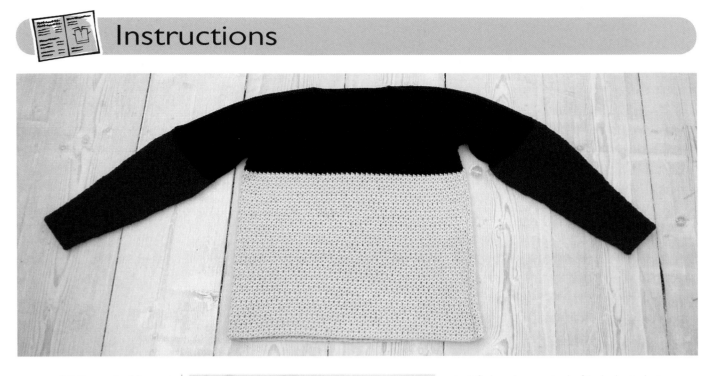

Abbreviations:

beg = beginning
ch = chain(s)
cm = centimetre(s)
cont = continue
dc = double crochet
dec = decrease
foll = follows
group = leaving last loop of each on hook work 3tr in centre of V st, yrh and draw through all 4 loops
inc = increase(d)
patt = pattern
rep = repeat
RS = right side
sp = space
ss = slip stitch
st(s) = stitch(es)
tog = together
tr = treble
tr2tog = (yrh, insert hook as indicated, yrh and draw loop through, yrh and draw through 2 loops) twice, yrh and draw through all 3 loops on hook
WS = wrong side
yrh = yarn round hook

BACK:

With 3.50mm (UK 9) hook and A, make 96[102:108:112]ch.

Foundation row: (WS) 1tr in 4th ch from hook, *miss next ch, (1tr, 1ch, 1tr – called V) into next ch, rep from * to last 2ch, miss next ch, 2tr in last ch, turn. 45[48:51:53] Vs.

Cont in patt as foll:

1st row: (RS) 3ch (counts as first tr), 1tr in st at base of ch, *1ch, 1 group in centre of next V, rep from * ending 1ch, leaving last loop of each on hook work 2tr in 3rd of 3ch, yrh and draw through all 3 loops on hook, turn.

2nd row: 3ch, (1tr, 1ch, 1tr) in first 1ch sp, *(1tr, 1ch, 1tr) in next 1ch sp, rep from * ending 1tr in 3rd of 3ch, turn. 46[49:52:54] Vs.

3rd row: 3ch, 1 group in centre of first V, *1ch, 1 group in centre of next V, rep from * ending 1tr in 3rd of 3ch, turn.

4th row: 3ch, 1tr in first tr, *(1tr, 1ch, 1tr) in next 1ch sp, rep from * ending 2tr in 3rd of 3ch, turn. 45[48:51:53] Vs. These 4 rows form patt. Rep them until work measures 37cm (14½in) from beg, ending with a 1st patt row. Cut off A and join in B.

Yoke:

Next row: (WS) With B, 3ch (counts as first tr), miss st at base of ch, 2tr in next tr, *1tr in 1ch sp, 1tr in next group, rep from * ending 1tr in last 1ch sp, 1tr in each of last 2tr, turn. 96[102:108:112]tr.

Next row: 3ch, miss st at base of ch, working in back loop of each st only, 1tr in each tr to end, working last tr in 3rd of 3ch, turn.

Rep last row 5 times more.

Shape for top of sleeves:
With 3.50mm (UK 9) hook and separate length of B, make 24ch, join with a ss in 3rd of 3ch at beg of last row. Fasten off.

Next row: Make 26ch, 1tr in 4th ch from hook, 1tr in each of next 22ch, patt across Back, then work 1tr in each of 24ch, turn. 144[150:156:160]tr.

Cont in tr, working in back loop only of each st, until yoke measures 24[24:25:25]cm (00[00:00:00]in) from beg, ending with a WS row. Fasten off.

Mark 59th[61st:63rd:64th] st from each end to denote shoulders.

FRONT:
Work as given for Back until 8 rows less than yoke have been worked, ending with a WS row.

Shape neck:
Next row: Patt 63[65:67:68] sts, tr2tog over next 2 sts, turn.

Dec 1tr at neck edge on next 5 rows.

59[61:63:64]tr.

Work 2 rows straight. Fasten off.

With RS of work facing, miss centre 14[16:18:20]tr at base of neck, rejoin yarn to next st, 3ch, miss st at base of ch, tr2tog over next 2 sts, patt to end, turn.

Dec 1tr at neck edge on next 5 rows.

59[61:63:64]tr. Work 2 rows straight. Fasten off.

SLEEVES: (make 2)
With 3.50mm (UK 9) hook and C, make 42[42:46:46]ch. Work foundation row as given for Back. 18[18:20:20]Vs.

Cont in patt as given for Back, work 3 rows.

Inc row: 3ch, 1tr in first tr, (1tr, 1ch, 1tr) in sp before first group, *(1tr, 1ch, 1tr) in next 1ch sp, rep from * ending (1tr, 1ch, 1tr) in sp after last group, 2tr in 3rd of 3ch, turn. 1 V inc at each end of row. Cont in patt, inc in this way on every foll 4th row until there are 34[34:36:36]Vs. Work 7 rows straight. Fasten off.

NECK EDGING:
With WS tog and front facing, join B to sleeve edge. With 3.50mm (UK 9) hook and working through both pieces, work 1dc in each tr to join top of sleeve seam and shoulder. Fasten off.

Now join B to neck edge and join other side in same way.

With 3.00mm (UK 11) hook and RS of work facing, join on B and work evenly around neck edge in dc, join with a ss into first dc. Work 1 more round in dc. Fasten off.

Making up

With WS tog, pin top of sleeves to sleeve edge of yoke. With sleeve facing, join on B and with 3.50mm (UK 9) hook, work a row of dc to join pieces tog, working 1dc in each group and each ch, turn.

Next row: 1dc in each dc to end. Fasten off.

Join other sleeve in same way. Join side and sleeve seams. Press seams.

Lace towel edging

Customise your plain towels with this decorative edging.

Worked in 4-ply cotton, this deep lace edging is based on a traditional pattern and consists of a series of distinctive scallops decorated with pretty picot points.

GETTING STARTED

★★ *Construction is unusual but easy to work once you have had some practice.*

Size:
13cm (5in) deep x 50cm (19½in) wide

How much yarn:
1 x 100g (3½oz) ball of Wendy Supreme Luxury Cotton 4-ply in White (shade 1820)

Hook:
2.50mm (UK 12) hook

Additional items:
White sewing thread and needle

Tension:
8 rows of edging measure approximately 8cm (3⅛in) on 2.50mm (UK 12) hook
IT IS ESSENTIAL TO WORK TO THE STATED TENSION TO ACHIEVE SUCCESS

What you have to do:
Work mainly in treble and chain. Work scallops over eight rows and edge them with picots. Work edging into chain loops at opposite edge to scallops and sew to towel.

The Yarn
Wendy Supreme Cotton 4-ply (approx. 267m/291 yards per 100g/3½oz ball) is 100% mercerized cotton. It has a tight twist and slight sheen ideal for lace edgings. It is machine-washable.

Instructions

Abbreviations:

ch = chain(s)
cm = centimetre(s)
dc = double crochet
htr = half treble
rep = repeat
sp = space
ss = slip stitch
tr = treble

EDGING:
First scallop:

With 2.50mm (UK 12) hook make 18ch firmly.

1st row: 2tr in 7th ch from hook, 2ch, 2tr in next ch, 5ch, miss 5ch, 2tr in next ch, 2ch, 2tr in next ch, miss last 3ch, turn.

2nd row: 6ch, (2tr, 2ch, 2tr) in first 2ch sp, 5ch, (2tr, 2ch, 2tr) in next 2ch sp, turn.

3rd row: 6ch, (2tr, 2ch, 2tr – called 1 shell) in first 2ch sp, 3ch, 1dc around 5ch bars of previous 2 rows, 3ch, 1 shell in next 2ch sp, turn.

4th row: 8ch, 1 shell in first 2ch sp, 5ch, 1 shell in next 2ch sp, turn.

5th row: 6ch, 1 shell in first 2ch sp, 5ch, 1 shell in next 2ch sp, 7tr in 8ch loop, 2ch, 7tr in same loop, ss in tr immediately before 6ch loop, 3ch (counts as 1tr), 1dc in same loop, turn.

6th row: Miss first tr of 7tr, 1tr in each of next 6tr, 1 shell in 2ch sp, 1tr in each of next 7tr, 1 shell in next 2ch sp, 3ch, 1dc around 5ch bars of previous 2 rows, 3ch, 1 shell in next 2ch sp, turn.

7th row: 6ch, 1 shell in first 2ch sp, 5ch, 1 shell in next 2ch sp, 1tr in first of 7tr, (2ch, miss one tr, 1tr in next tr) 4 times, (2ch, 1tr) twice in 2ch sp, 2ch, 1tr in next tr, (2ch, miss one tr, 1tr in next tr) 4 times, 1dc in last of 3ch left at end of 1st row, turn.

8th row: 3ch, 1dc in first ch sp, * 2ch, 1tr in next ch sp, (4ch, 1dc in top of tr just worked – called 1 picot, 1tr in same sp) 3 times, 2ch, 1dc in next sp, rep from * 4 times more, 4ch, 1 shell in next 2ch sp, 5ch, 1 shell in next 2ch sp, turn.

Second scallop:

9th row: As 3rd row.

10th row: As 2nd row.

11th row: As 2nd row.

12th row: 8ch, 1 shell in 2ch sp, 3ch, 1dc around 5ch bars of previous 2 rows, 3ch, 1 shell in next 2ch sp, turn.

13th row: As 5th row.

14th row: Miss first of 7tr, 1tr in each of next 6tr, 1 shell in 2ch sp, 1tr in each of next 7tr, 1 shell in next 2ch sp, 5ch, 1 shell in next 2ch sp, turn.

15th row: 6ch, 1 shell in 2ch sp, 3ch, 1dc around 5ch bars of previous 2 rows, 3ch, 1 shell in next 2ch sp, 1tr in first of 7tr, (2ch, miss one tr, 1tr in next tr) 4 times, (2ch, 1tr) twice in 2ch sp, 2ch, 1tr in next tr, (2ch, miss one tr, 1tr in next tr) 4 times, turn.

16th row: 2ch, 1tr in 2nd ch sp, 2ch, ss in last picot of previous scallop, 1dc in top of tr just worked, in same sp

work 1tr, (1 picot, 1tr) twice, *2ch, 1dc in next sp, 2ch, in next sp work 1tr, (1 picot, 1tr) 3 times, rep from * 3 times more, 2ch, 1dc in next sp, 4ch, 1 shell in next 2ch sp**, 5ch, 1 shell in next 2ch sp, turn.

Third scallop:

17th row: As 2nd row.

18th row: As 3rd row.

19th row: As 2nd row.

20th row: As 4th row.

21st row: 6ch, 1 shell in first 2ch sp, 3ch, 1dc around 5ch bars of previous 2 rows, 3ch (counts as 1tr), 1 shell in next 2ch sp, 7tr in 8ch loop, 2ch, 7tr in same loop, ss in tr immediately before 6ch loop, 3ch, 1dc in same loop, turn.

22nd row: As 14th row.

23rd row: 6ch, 1 shell in first 2ch sp, 5ch, 1 shell in next 2ch sp, 1tr in first of 7tr, (2ch, miss one tr, 1tr in next tr) 4 times, (2ch, 1tr) twice in 2ch sp, 2ch, 1tr in next tr, (2ch, miss one tr, 1tr in next tr) 4 times, turn.

24th row: As 16th row to **, 3ch, 1dc around 5ch bars of previous 2 rows, 3ch, 1 shell in next 2ch sp, turn.

25th row: 6ch, 1 shell in next 2ch sp, 5ch, 1 shell in next 2ch sp, turn. Rep 2nd–6th rows.

Next row: As 7th row but omit last dc.

Next row: As 16th row. Rep 9th–24th rows.

49th row: 6ch, 1dc in first 2ch sp, 6ch, 1dc in next 2ch sp. Fasten off.

Edging:

1st row: With whichever side you prefer to be 'wrong side' facing, join yarn in first loop of top edge, 1dc in this loop, (4ch, 1dc in next loop) to end, turn.

2nd row: 2ch, (5dc in next ch sp, 1dc in next dc) to last ch sp, 5dc in last ch sp, 1htr in last dc. Fasten off.

Making up

Darn in ends. Damp press to shape and to length. Pin edging to towel hemline. Using white sewing thread, attach edging by back stitching around each stitch underneath chain edge of last row of dc. Turn towel over and catch down crochet along fold of towel hem.

Gingham shopping bag

Check out the shops with an appropriately checked bag!

This bag with long handles is worked in a three-colour gingham pattern in off-beat colours. For additional strength, it is lined with furnishing fabric with a printed pattern.

GETTING STARTED

⭐⭐ *Check pattern needs practice but requires no shaping; lining requires some simple sewing skills.*

Size:
Bag measures 41cm (16in) wide x 29.5cm (11½in) tall, excluding handles

How much yarn:
6 x 50g (1¾oz) balls of Debbie Bliss Cotton DK in colour A – White (shade 01)
3 balls in each of two colours: B – Pale Green (shade 20) and C – Apple Green (shade 55)

Hook:
4.00mm (UK 8) crochet hook

Additional items:
85 x 65cm (33½ x 25½in) rectangle of furnishing-weight cotton fabric in toning colours
White sewing cotton

Tension:
16 sts and 9 rows measure 10cm (4in) square over patt on 4.00mm (UK 8) hook
IT IS ESSENTIAL TO WORK TO THE STATED TENSION TO ACHIEVE SUCCESS

What you have to do:
Work check pattern in trebles using three colours. Use two colours in each row, working over colour not in use. Sew fabric lining for bag.

The Yarn
Debbie Bliss Cotton DK (approx. 84m/92 yards per 50g/1¾oz ball) contains 100% cotton. It produces a strong fabric with a matt finish that can be machine washed. There is a good range of colours.

Instructions

Note:
When working check patt, always join in new colour on last part of last st in old colour and work sts over yarn not in use.

BAG:
With 4.00mm (UK 8) hook and A, make 132ch, join with a ss into first ch to form a ring, making sure that ch is not twisted. Cont in rounds of tr and check patt as foll:

1st round: With A, 3ch (counts as first tr), 1tr into each of next 2ch, *with B, 1tr into each of next 3ch, with A, 1tr into each of foll 3ch, rep from * to last 3ch, with B, 1tr into each last 3ch, join in C on last tr, join with a ss into 3rd of 3ch.

2nd round: With C, 3ch, miss st at base of ch, 1tr into each of next 2tr, *with A, 1tr into each of next 3tr, with C, 1tr into each of foll 3tr, rep from * to last 3 sts, with A, 1tr into each of last 3tr, join with a ss into 3rd of 3ch.

3rd round: As 2nd, but joining in A on last tr.

4th round: With A, 3ch, miss st at base of ch, 1tr into each of next 2tr, *with B, 1tr into each of next 3tr, with A, 1tr into each of foll 3tr, rep from * to last 3 sts, with B, 1tr into each of last 3tr, join with a ss into 3rd of 3ch.

5th round: As 4th, but joining in C on last tr. The 2nd–5th rounds form patt. Rep them 5 times more, then work 2nd and 3rd rounds again. Fasten off.

HANDLES: (make 2)
With 4.00mm (UK 8) hook and A, make 90ch.

Foundation row: (RS) 1tr into 4th ch from hook, 1tr into each ch to end, turn. 88tr.

Next row: 3ch (counts as first tr), miss tr at base of ch, 1tr into each tr to end, working last tr into 3rd of 3ch, turn. Rep last row once more. Fasten off.

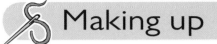

Making up

Lining:

From cotton fabric, cut: 2 handle pieces, 7 x 60cm (2¾ x 24in); 2 bases, 13 x 35cm (5 x 14in); 1 lining piece, 35 x 85cm (14in x 33½in). With RS facing, pin two short sides of lining tog and machine-stitch, taking a 2cm (¾in) seam allowance. Press seam open. Fold and press under a double 2cm (¾in) turning around top edge. With RS facing, pin one base to lower edge of lining, making 1.5cm (⅝in) snips into lining where it meets corners so that base will lie flat. Tack in place, then machine-stitch taking a 2cm (¾in) seam allowance. Press under a 2cm (¾in) turning along each long edge of handle backings. With WS facing, pin each one centrally to one crochet handle. Adjust pressure on your machine's presser foot to lightest setting and set stitch length to 3mm (⅛in). Top-stitch lining to handles, working a line of machine-stitch 3mm (⅛in) in from each long edge.

Fold top of lining in half in line with centre of short edges of base and mark these two points with a pin. Now measure from points on top edge 11.5cm (4½in) in from each of the two pins and mark each one with a pin. Remove first two pins.

With RS facing outwards and WS of handles to WS of lining, pin ends of handles to top edge of lining so that outside edges line up with four marker pins. Allow a 1.5cm (⅝in) overlap and tack ends in place securely. Press under a 2cm (¾in) turning along each edge of second base piece. Unfold and mitre corners, then re-press. With RS facing, pin base to bottom of bag. Slip stitch folded edge of fabric to edge of crochet. Machine-stitch 5mm (¼in) in from edge, easing fullness of crochet around each corner as you stitch.

Turn bag RS out and with WS tog slip lining inside. Adjust so that base corners are in line, then pin top edges together, easing crochet in slightly so that they fit together properly. Machine-stitch 5mm (¼in) from top edge.

Striped beach poncho

Slip this poncho on over shorts and head for a barbecue on the beach.

In broad patterned stripes and deckchair colours, this rectangular poncho with fringed edges is easy to throw on when the weather changes.

GETTING STARTED

Once you are familiar with the pattern, it is easy to keep correct but pay attention to front neck shaping.

Size:
Actual width: 96cm (38in)
Length from shoulder: 50cm (20in)

How much yarn:
7 x 50g (1¾oz) balls of Debbie Bliss Cotton DK in each of three colours: A – Light Green (shade 60); B – Red (shade 47) and C – Dark Green (shade 39)

Hook:
4.00mm (UK 8) crochet hook

Tension:
17 sts measure 10cm (4in) and 9 rows measure 8cm (3⅛in) over patt on 4.00mm (UK 8) hook
IT IS ESSENTIAL TO WORK TO THE STATED TENSION TO ACHIEVE SUCCESS

What you have to do:
Make poncho in two identical pieces working from side edge to centre. Work throughout in striped pattern with rows of mesh, crossed trebles and double crochet. Divide work and shape front neckline as directed. Work double crochet edging around outer edge. Knot fringe through lower edge of front and back.

Instructions

The Yarn
Debbie Bliss Cotton DK (approx. 84m/ 92 yards per 50g/ 1¾oz ball) contains 100% cotton. This soft yarn produces a strong machine-washable fabric in a wide range of exciting shades.

Notes: Pattern for poncho is reversible. Always join in new colour on last part of last st worked in old colour.

PONCHO:
Right side:
With 4.00mm (UK 8) hook and A, make 170ch.
Foundation row: 1tr into 6th ch from hook, *1ch, miss 1ch, 1tr into next ch, rep from * to end, turn. 167 sts; 83 blocks.
1st row: With A, 4ch (counts as 1tr, 1ch), miss first ch sp, work 2 crossed tr as foll: 1tr forward into next ch sp, working behind forward tr, 1tr back into missed sp, *1tr forward into next free sp, 1tr back into sp previously

Abbreviations:
ch = chain
cm = centimetre(s)
dc = double crochet
dc2tog = (insert hook where given, yrh and draw loop through) twice, yrh and draw through all 3 loops
dtr = double treble
foll = follow(s)(ing)
patt = pattern
rep = repeat(s)
RS = right side
sp(s) = space(s)
ss = slip stitch
st(s) = stitch(es)
tr = treble
tr2tog = (yrh, insert hook where given, yrh and draw loop through, yrh and draw through 2 loops) twice, yrh and draw through all 3 loops;
yrh = yarn round hook

worked into, rep from * to end, ending 1tr forward into sp formed by turning ch, 1tr back into sp previously worked into, 1tr into 4th of 5ch, (on foll reps work into 3rd of 4ch), turn.

2nd row: With A, 1ch (counts as first dc), miss st at base of ch, 1dc into each st, ending 1dc into each of 4th and 3rd of 4ch, turn. 167 sts. Cut off A.

3rd row: With B, 4ch (counts as 1tr, 1ch), miss st at base of ch, miss next st, 1tr into next st, *1ch, miss next st, 1tr into next st, rep from * to end, working last tr into 1ch, turn.
167 sts; 83 blocks.

4th and 5th rows: With B, as 1st and 2nd rows. Cut off B.

6th row: With C, as 3rd row.

7th and 8th rows: With C, as 1st and 2nd rows. Cut off C.

9th row: With A, as 3rd row. These 9 rows form patt. Work a further 32 rows in patt, so ending with a 5th patt row.

Shape front neck:
Keep colour sequence correct.

1st row: 4ch, (counts as 1tr, 1ch), miss st at base of ch, miss next st, (1tr into next st, 1ch, miss next st) 38 times, tr2tog over next 2 sts, turn. 79 sts.

2nd row: 4ch, (does not count as a st), tr2tog over first 2 sps, 1tr forward into next ch sp, 1tr back into same sp as 2nd leg of tr2tog, patt to end, turn. 76 sts.

3rd row: 1ch, (counts as 1dc), miss st at base of ch, 1dc into each of next 72 sts, dc2tog over next 2sts, turn. 74 sts.

4th row: 3ch, (does not count as a st), miss first 3 sts, 1tr into next st, (1ch, miss next st, 1tr into next st)
35 times working last tr into 1ch, turn. 71 sts.

5th row: 4ch, patt 32 pairs of crossed tr as set, work one more pair of crossed tr working 1tr forward as set then leaving last loop of each st on hook work 1tr back into sp previously worked into, 1tr into next tr and 1dtr into foll tr, yrh and draw through all
4 loops, turn. 68 sts.

6th row: 1ch (does not count as a st), miss st at base of ch, dc2tog over next 2 sts, 1dc into each st to end, ending 1dc into 4th and 3rd turning ch, turn. 66 sts.

7th row: 4ch, miss st at base of ch, miss next st, (1tr into next st, 1ch, miss next st) 30 times, leaving last loop of each on hook work 1tr into next st, miss next st, 1tr into next st and 1dtr into next st, yrh and draw through all 4 loops, turn. 63 sts.

8th row: as 2nd row. 60 sts.

9th row: 1ch (counts as 1dc), miss st at base of ch, 1dc into each of next

56 sts, dc2tog over next 2sts, turn. 58 sts.

10th row: 3ch (does not count as a st), miss first 3 sts, 1tr into next st, (1ch, miss next st, 1tr into next st) 27 times, working last tr into turning ch, turn. 55 sts.

11th row: With C, 1ch (counts as 1dc), miss st at base of ch, (1dc into ch sp, 1dc into next tr) 26 times, dc2tog over ch sp and last tr. 54 sts. Fasten off.

Back neck:
Return to last row before front neck shaping, miss 8 sts and rejoin C to next st, 4ch (counts as 1tr, 1ch), miss st at base of ch and next st, 1tr into next st, patt to end, turn. 79 sts.

Patt 9 rows.

Next row: With C, 1ch, miss st at base of ch, 1dc into each st and ch sp to end. Fasten off.

Left side:
Work as given for Right side.

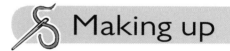

Making up

Sew right and left side of poncho together at centre front and back.

Main edging:
With 4.00mm (UK 8) hook and RS facing, join C to one outer corner, 1ch (counts as first dc), work in dc evenly all round outer edges working alternately 5dc into row ends of one 3-row stripe and 4dc into row-ends of next 3-row stripe, 1dc into each ch sp and base of tr along side edges and 2dc into each corner, join with a ss into first ch.

Next round: 1ch, miss st at base of ch, 1dc into each dc all round, working 2dc into each corner, join with a ss into first ch. Fasten off.

Neck edging:
With 4.00mm (UK 8) hook and RS facing, join C to neck edge at top of centre back seam, 1ch (counts as first dc), work in dc evenly around neck edge, join with a ss into first ch.

Next round: 1ch, miss st at base of ch, 1dc into each dc to 2dc before centre front, (dc2tog over next 2sts) twice, 1dc into each dc to end, join with a ss into first ch. Fasten off.

Fringe:
Cut 14cm (5½in) lengths of A, B and C. For each tassel, use 4 strands of one colour. Alternating tassel colours, fold strands in half and knot first tassel into corner st on lower edge, *miss 3dc and knot a tassel into next st on lower edge, rep from * to corner.

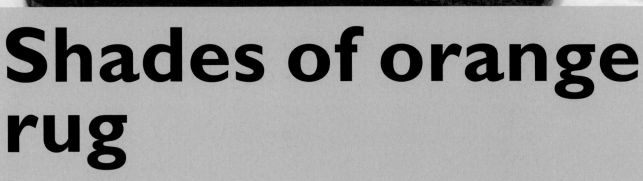

Shades of orange rug

Three different toning colours are shaded together to make this retro-style rug.

The dense tweedy texture of this rug is enhanced by subtle shading, achieved by joining in the new yarn gradually along with the old one.

The Yarn

Debbie Bliss Luxury Tweed Chunky (approx. 100m/109 yards per 100g/3½oz ball) is a blend of 90% wool and 10% angora. Hand-wash only, it produces a luxurious and thick fabric with subtle slubs of colour, which create a tweedy effect.

GETTING STARTED

Basic fabric with no shaping but care is needed with yarn colour changes for the shaded effect.

Size:
64 x 90cm (25 x 35½in)

How much yarn:
2 x 100g (3½oz) hanks of Debbie Bliss Luxury Tweed Chunky in each of three colours: A – Dark Red (shade 20); B – Bright Red (shade 07); C – Orange (shade 09)

Hook:
7.00mm (UK 2) crochet hook

Tension:
10 sts and 8 rows measure 10cm (4in) square over htr on 7.00mm (UK 2) hook
IT IS ESSENTIAL TO WORK TO THE STATED TENSION TO ACHIEVE SUCCESS

What you have to do:
Read instructions at start of rug to wind hanks into balls as specified. Read note on joining in new yarn – split two colours and work with both together for a while to achieve a subtle, random change of colour. Work throughout in rows of half trebles. Work edging around rug in rounds of double crochet.

Instructions

Abbreviations:

approx = approximately
beg = beginning
ch = chain
cm = centimetre(s)
cont = continue
dc = double crochet
foll = following
htr = half treble
m = metres
rep = repeat
RS = right side
sp = space
ss = slip stitch
st(s) = stitch(es)
WS = wrong side

Note:

New yarn can be joined at beg or at any point in a row. When joining in new yarn, work until there is approx 6m of old ball of yarn left, carefully split the two strands and discard one of them. Mark out 6.5m (7 yards) at the start of new ball of yarn and split this in two, also discarding one of them. Cont combining the two split lengths of old and new yarns. Do not worry if yarn breaks where it is split – simply knot ends together and keep working. Any knots will be hidden in the stitches or can be sewn in when the rug is complete.

RUG:

Before you start, wind one hank of each shade into large balls; wind remaining hank of each into 2 balls of equal weight. With 7.00mm (UK 2) hook and large ball of A, make 62ch.

Foundation row: (RS) 1htr into 3rd ch from hook, 1htr into each ch to end, turn. 60 sts.

1st row: 2ch (does not count as a st), 1htr into each htr to end, omitting turning ch, turn.

Rep last row until there is approx 6.5m (7 yards) of yarn left. Foll instructions on joining yarn, join in and cont with large ball of B. Cont until there is approx 6.5m (7 yards) of yarn left and then join in and cont with large ball of C.

Cont until there is approx 6.5m (7 yards) of yarn left and then join in small ball of A. When there is approx 6m of yarn left, join in small ball of B; when there is approx 6.5m (7 yards) of yarn left, join in small ball of C; when there is approx 6.5m (7 yards) of yarn left, join in small ball of A. Cont in A until rug measures approx 86cm (34in) from beg, ending with a WS row.

Edging:

Note: Cont with A until it runs out and then work part rounds with B and C to enhance random effect.

1st round: 2ch, 1dc into each htr to end, 2ch (for corner), working evenly in dc (working approx 4dc to every 3 row-ends) along side edge of rug, 2ch, 1dc into each loop along other side of foundation row, 2ch, work evenly in dc along other side edge, join with a ss into 2ch sp.

2nd and 3rd rounds: Work (1dc, 2ch, 1dc) into 2ch sp at each corner and 1dc into each dc of previous round, join with a ss into first dc. Fasten off.

Beaded curtain

This summer-style curtain looks great on a kitchen door.

Have fun making this door curtain. The colourful beaded strands hang from a filet crochet pelmet that has an antique lace effect.

The Yarn

King Cole Craft Cotton (approx. 133m/145 yards per 100g/3½oz ball) contains 90% cotton and 10% other fibres. It is a strong, hardwearing yarn, good for craft projects. It is white or natural in colour.

GETTING STARTED

★★★ *Working the pelmet requires concentration but making the beaded strands is fun.*

Size:

Pelmet measures 76cm (30in) across x 22cm (8½in) deep; short strands measure approximately 135cm (53in) long

How much yarn:

2 x 100g (3½oz) balls of King Cole Craft Cotton in Natural (shade 46)

Hook:

6.00mm (UK 4) crochet hook

Additional items:

100 round wooden beads (10 x 8mm/ ⅜ x ⁷/₁₆in) in

each of natural, aqua and green
50 round wooden beads (8 x 6mm/ ⁷/₁₆ x ¼in) in aqua
Tapestry needle

Tension:

Measurement across 12th patt row is 20cm (8in) and 1 patt rep (12 rows) measures 17cm (6¾in) over patt on 6.00mm (UK 4) hook
IT IS ESSENTIAL TO WORK TO THE STATED TENSION TO ACHIEVE SUCCESS

What you have to do:

Work pelmet starting at one short end and shaping pointed edge as given. Work border along short ends and long straight edge. Thread beads onto yarn and work beaded strands. Sew beaded strands at intervals along pointed edge.

Instructions

Abbreviations:

beg = beginning
ch = chain
cm = centimetre(s)
dc = double crochet
foll = following
patt = pattern
rep = repeat
RS = right side
sp(s) = space(s)
ss = slip stitch
st(s) = stitches
tr = treble
WS = wrong side

PELMET:

With 6.00mm (UK 4) hook make 38ch.

Foundation row: (RS) 1tr in 4th ch from hook, (1tr in each of next 2ch, 5ch, miss 5ch, 1dc in each of next 3ch, 5ch, miss 5ch, 1tr in each of next 2ch) twice, turn.

1st row: 3ch, miss st at base of ch, 1tr in next tr, 3tr in 5ch sp, 4ch, miss 1dc, 1dc in next dc, 4ch, 3tr in 5ch sp, 1tr in next tr, 3ch, miss next 2tr, 1tr in next tr, 3tr in 5ch sp, 4ch, miss 1dc, 1dc in next dc, 4ch, 3tr in 5ch sp, 1tr in next tr, turn.

2nd row: 1ss in each of first 4tr, 3ch, 3tr in 4ch sp, 2ch, 3tr in next 4ch sp, 1tr in next tr, 4ch, miss 3tr and 1ch, 1dc in next ch, 4ch, miss 3tr, 1tr in next tr, 3tr in 4ch sp, 2ch, 3tr in next 4ch sp, 1tr in next tr, 4ch, miss 3tr, 1dc in top of turning ch, turn.

3rd row: 8ch, miss 1dc, 4ch and 3tr, 1tr in next tr, 2tr in 2ch sp, 1tr in next tr, 5ch, miss 3tr and 3ch, 1dc in next ch, 1dc in next dc, 1dc in next ch, 5ch, miss next 3tr, 1tr in next tr, 2tr in 2ch sp, 1tr in next tr, turn.

4th row: 1ss in each of first 4tr, 3ch, 3tr in 5ch sp, 4ch, miss 1dc, 1dc in next dc, 4ch, 3tr in 5ch sp, 1tr in next tr, 3ch, miss 2tr, 1tr in next tr, 3tr in 8ch sp, 4ch, 1tr in 6th of 8ch, turn.

5th row: 3ch, 3tr in 4ch sp, 1tr in next tr, 4ch, miss 3tr and 1ch, 1dc in next ch, 4ch, miss 3tr, 1tr in next tr, 3tr in 4ch sp, 2ch, 3tr in next 4ch sp, 1tr in next tr, turn.

6th row: 1ss in each of first 4tr, 3ch, 2tr in 2ch sp, 1tr in next tr, 5ch, miss 3tr and 3ch, 1dc in next ch, 1dc in next dc, 1dc in next ch, 5ch, miss 3tr, 1tr in next tr, 1tr in top of turning ch, turn.

7th row: 3ch, miss st at base of ch, 1tr in next tr, 3tr in 5ch sp, 4ch, miss 1dc, 1dc in next dc, 4ch, 3tr in 5ch sp, 1tr in next tr, 6ch, 1ss in top of turning ch, 5ch, turn, miss first 3ch, 1tr in each of next 2ch, 1ss in 3rd of 6ch, turn, 1ss in each of last 4 sts, turn.

8th row: 5ch, miss first 3ch, 1tr in each of next 2ch, 1tr in first ss, 4ch, miss next 3 sts and first of 3ch, 1dc in next ch, 4ch, miss 3tr, 1tr in next tr, 3tr in 4ch sp, 2ch, 3tr in next 4ch sp, 1tr in next tr, 4ch, 1dc in top of turning ch, turn.

9th row: 8ch, miss 1dc, 4ch and 3tr, 1tr in next tr, 2tr in 2ch sp, 1tr in next tr, 5ch, miss 3tr and 3ch, 1dc in next ch, 1dc in next dc, 1dc in next ch, 8ch, 1ss in top of turning ch, 5ch, turn, miss first 3ch, 1tr in each of next 2ch, 1ss in 3rd of 8ch, turn, 1ss in each of last 4 sts, turn.

10th row: 5ch, miss first 3ch, 1tr in each

of next 2ch, 1tr in first ss, 3ch, miss next 2ss, 1tr in next ss, 3tr in 5ch sp, 4ch, miss 1dc, 1dc in next dc, 4ch, 3tr in next 5ch sp, 1tr in next tr, 3ch, miss 2tr, 1tr in next tr, 3tr in 8ch sp, 1ch, 1dc in 6th of 8ch, turn.

11th row: 3ch, 3tr in first sp, 1tr in next tr, 4ch, miss 3tr and 1ch, 1dc in next ch, 4ch, miss 3tr, 1tr in next tr, 3tr in 4ch sp, 2ch, 3tr in next 4ch sp, 1tr in next tr, 4ch, miss 3tr and 1ch, 1dc in next ch, 7ch, 1ss in top of turning ch, 5ch, turn, miss first 3ch, 1tr in each of next 2ch, 1ss in 3rd of 7ch, turn, 1ss in each of last 4 sts, turn.

12th row: 5ch, miss first 3ch, 1tr in each of next 2ch, 1tr in first ss, 5ch, miss next 3ss and 3ch, 1dc in next ch, 1dc in next dc, 1dc in next ch, 5ch, miss 3tr, 1tr in next tr, 2tr in 2ch sp, 1tr in next tr, 5ch, miss 3tr and 3ch, 1dc in next ch, 1dc in next dc, 1dc in next ch, 5ch, miss 3tr, 1tr in next tr, 1tr in top of turning ch, turn.

1st to 12th rows form patt. Rep 1st to 12th rows 3 times more. Fasten off.

Border:

1st row: With 6.00mm (UK 4) hook and RS facing, rejoin yarn to top of turning ch at beg of final row, 3ch, 1tr in each tr or ch to end of final row working 3tr in last st, work in tr along long straight edge taking care to keep work flat, 3tr in end st, 1tr in each ch along short end, turn.

2nd row: 3ch, miss st at base of ch, (1tr in each tr to centre of 3tr at corner, 3tr in centre tr) twice, 1tr in each tr to end, 1tr in top of turning ch. Fasten off.

CURTAIN:

Long beaded strand: (make 4)
Thread 15 random beads onto ball of yarn, then to make weighted end thread 7 beads in foll order – small aqua, green, natural, large aqua, natural, green and small aqua, miss final bead and thread yarn back through next 6 beads, fasten off short end securely. Make a loop in yarn immediately above last bead and make 20ch, *remove hook, enlarge working loop and pass ball of yarn and beads through working loop, tighten working loop, slide 3 beads along yarn and up to last ch worked, make a loop in yarn immediately above bead, make 40ch, rep from * 4 times more, working 20ch not 40ch at end of last rep. Fasten off leaving a 30cm (12in) tail.

Short beaded strand: (make 13)
Thread 12 random beads onto ball of yarn, then to make weighted end thread 7 beads in foll order – small aqua, green, natural, large aqua, natural, green and small aqua, miss final bead and thread yarn back through next 6 beads, fasten off short end securely. * Make a loop in yarn immediately above last bead and make 40ch, remove hook, enlarge working loop and pass ball of yarn and beads through working loop, tighten working loop, slide 3 beads along yarn and up to last ch worked, rep from * 3 times more, make a loop in yarn immediately above last bead and make 10ch. Fasten off leaving a 30cm (12in) tail. Sew beaded strands to shaped edge of pelmet – one long beaded strand to end of shortest row of each rep (6th patt row). Miss one row at each side of shortest row and sew one short beaded strand to next row at each side (4th and 8th patt rows). Sew one short beaded strand to end of foundation row and one to end of longest row of each rep (12th patt row).

Round and square cushion pair

Team these bright cushions together and make a statement on your sofa.

This mix 'n' match cushion set consists of a circular cushion in one-round stripes and a square cushion with blocks of colours.

The Yarn

King Cole Merino Blend DK (approx. 112m/122 yards per 50g/1¾oz ball) contains 100% pure wool in a superwash format, which means it is very practical. The wide range of shades allows for striking colour combinations.

GETTING STARTED

Only one basic stitch is used but a good finished result relies on neat, careful work and making up.

Size:

Round cushion: 40cm (16in) in diameter

Square cushion: 40cm (16in) square

How much yarn:

Round cushion:

1 x 50g (1¾oz) ball of King Cole Merino Blend DK in each of five colours: A – Linden (shade 165); B – Sugar Pink (shade 797); C – Scarlet (shade 9); D – Gold (shade 55); E – Saxe (shade 859)

Square cushion:

2 x 50g (1¾oz) balls of King Cole Merino Blend DK in each of four colours: A – Linden (shade 165); B – Sugar Pink (shade 797); C – Scarlet (shade 9); E – Saxe (shade 859)

1 ball in colour D – Gold (shade 55)

Hook:

4.00mm (UK 8) crochet hook

Additional items:

Sewing needle and matching thread

Round cushion: Circular cushion pad 40cm (16in) in diameter, Zip fastener 56cm (22in) long

Square cushion: Cushion pad 40cm (16in) square, 4 buttons

Tension:

17 sts and 14 rows measure 10cm (4in) square over htr on 4.00mm (UK 8) hook

IT IS ESSENTIAL TO WORK TO THE STATED TENSION TO ACHIEVE SUCCESS

What you have to do:

Work throughout in half trebles. Working each round in a different colour, make round cushion in rounds, increasing at regular intervals on rounds as directed. Make four square blocks in different colours for each of back and front of square cushion; positioning blocks as directed, sew them together. Crochet both cushions together around outer edge with half trebles. Sew a zip fastener into round cushion and make a back opening as described for square cushion.

![instructions icon] Instructions

Abbreviations:

beg = beginning
ch = chain(s)
cm = centimetre(s)
cont = continue
foll = following
htr = half treble
inc = increasing
rem = remaining
rep = repeat
RS = right side
ss = slip stitch
st(s) = stitch(es)
tog = together
WS = wrong side

ROUND CUSHION: FRONT & BACK:

(Alike)
With 4.00mm (UK 8) hook and A, make a magic circle (see how in Note on page 46).

Foundation round: 2ch (counts as first htr), 9htr into ring, change to B, join with a ss in 2nd of 2ch and tighten hole at centre. 10 sts.

1st round: 2ch, (1htr in next htr, 2htr in foll htr) 4 times, 1htr in next htr, 1htr in same st as 2ch, change to C, join with a ss in 2nd of 2ch. 15 sts.

2nd round: 2ch, (1htr in each of next 2htr, 2htr in foll htr) 4 times, 1htr in each of next 2htr, 1htr in same st as 2ch, change to D, join with a ss in 2nd of 2ch. 20 sts.

3rd round: 2ch, (1htr in next htr, 2htr in foll htr) 9 times, 1htr in next htr, 1htr in same st as 2ch, change to E, join with a ss in 2nd of 2ch. 30 sts.

4th round: 2ch, (1htr in each of next 2htr, 2htr in foll htr) 9 times, 1htr in each of next 2htr, 1htr in same st as 2ch, change to A, join with a ss in 2nd of 2ch. 40 sts.

5th round: 2ch, 1htr in each htr to end, change to B, join with a ss in 2nd of 2ch.

6th round: 2ch, (1htr in each of next 3htr, 2htr in foll htr) 9 times, 1htr in each of next 3htr, 1htr in same st as 2ch, change to C, join with a ss in 2nd of 2ch. 50 sts.

7th round: 2ch, (1htr in each of next 4htr, 2htr in foll htr) 9 times, 1htr in each of next 4htr, 1htr in same st as 2ch, change to D, join with a ss in 2nd of 2ch. 60 sts.

8th round: 2ch, 1htr in each htr to end, change to E, join with a ss in 2nd of 2ch.

9th round: 2ch, (1htr in each of next 5htr, 2htr in foll htr) 9 times, 1htr in each of next 5htr, 1htr in same st as 2ch, change to A, join with a ss in 2nd of 2ch. 70 sts.

10th round: 2ch, (1htr in each of next 6htr, 2htr in foll htr) 9 times, 1htr in each of next 6htr, 1htr in same st as 2ch, change to B, join with a ss in 2nd of 2ch. 80 sts.

11th–28th rounds: Cont in this way for another 18 rounds, working 1 round straight, then inc 10 sts on each of foll 2 rounds while working colours in alphabetical order, so ending with final round in D and 200 sts. Fasten off.

Zip edging and seam:
With 4.00mm (UK 8) hook and RS facing, join E to outer edge of Back, make 2ch, work 1htr in each of next 89 htr. Fasten off. Rep with Front but do not fasten off. Hold Back and Front with WS tog and zip edging matching and work 1htr through rem htr of both edges all around until all htr have been worked and pieces are joined, ss to beg of zip edging. Fasten off.

SQUARE CUSHION:
Square: (make 2 in each of A, B, C and E – 8 squares in total)
With 4.00mm (UK 8) hook make 35ch.
Foundation row: (RS) 1htr in 3rd ch from hook, 1htr in each ch to end, turn. 34 sts.
Next row: 2ch (counts as first htr), miss st at base of ch, 1htr in each htr to end, working last htr in 2nd of 2ch, turn. Work a further 26 rows in htr. Fasten off.

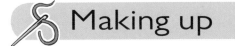 Making up

ROUND CUSHION:
Pin zip fastener between two open edges of zip edging and, using a sewing needle and matching thread, sew zip in place.

SQUARE CUSHION:
Front: Sew squares tog in foll formation:
Top left – B – with rows horiozontally.
Top right – C – with rows vertically.
Bottom left – E – with rows vertically.
Bottom right – A – with rows horizontally.
Back: Top half: Sew squares tog in foll formation:
Top left – C – with rows vertically.
Top right – B – with rows horizontally.
Bottom half: Sew squares tog in foll formation:
Bottom left – A – with rows horizontally.
Bottom right – E – with rows vertically.
Button band:
With 4.00mm (UK 8) hook and RS facing, join D to right-hand top corner of E square, make 2ch, work 69htr along top edge of E and A squares. Fasten off.
Buttonhole band:
With 4.00mm (UK 8) hook and RS facing, join D to left-hand bottom corner of C square, make 2ch, work 69htr along bottom edge of C and B squares, turn.
Buttonhole row: 2ch, miss st at base of ch, 1htr in each of next 10htr, 1ch, miss 1htr, (1htr in each of next 15htr, 1ch, miss 1htr) 3 times, 1htr in each of next 10htr, turn. Work 1 further row in htr, working 1htr in each 1ch. Fasten off.
Seam:
Hold Front and Back with WS tog and with top half of Back overlapping bottom half and pin in place around all 4 sides. With 4.00mm (UK 8) hook and RS of front facing, join D to side edge level with buttonhole band, make 2ch, work 1htr through all layers to join and create a seam, working 69htr along each side and 3htr in each corner, join with a ss in 2nd of 2ch. Fasten off. Sew buttons to button band to correspond with buttonholes.

Summer tote bag

Accessorize your summer outfits with this straw-like bag.

Ideal as a summer bag, this one is worked in a raffia-like yarn and basic double crochet fabric. The handles are strengthened with an inner core and sewn onto the outside of the bag at the top edge.

GETTING STARTED

 Easy basic fabric but working in rounds requires concentration especially as there is shaping throughout.

Size:
Bag is approximately 30cm (12in) wide at base, 45cm (18in) wide at top and 34cm (13¼in) high, excluding handles

How much yarn:
8 x 25g (1oz) skeins of Adriafil Rafia in Straw (shade 67)

Hook:
5.00mm (UK 6) crochet hook

Additional Items:
Sticky tape
128cm (46in) of clear plastic tubing, 5mm (¼in) in diameter

Tension:
12 sts and 15 rounds measure 10cm (4in) square over dc on 5.00mm (UK 6) hook
IT IS ESSENTIAL TO WORK TO THE STATED TENSION TO ACHIEVE SUCCESS

What you have to do:
Work thoughout in rounds of double crochet. Make oval base and shape sides of bag to give slightly flared shape. Make strips of double crochet fabric for handles and use to enclose lengths of plastic tubing for additional strength. Sew handles securely to top of bag.

The Yarn
Adriafil Rafia contains 100% wood pulp. This smooth flat raffia-style yarn is perfect for crochet, especially bags, hats and mats.

 Instructions

BAG:
Base:
With 5.00mm (UK 6) hook make 25ch.

Foundation round: 1dc in 2nd ch from hook, 1dc in each of next 22ch, 3dc in last ch, then work back in opposite side of ch as foll: 1dc in each of next 22ch, 2dc in last ch, join with a ss into first dc. 50 sts.

1st round: 1ch (does not count as a st), 2dc in first dc, 1dc in each of next 22dc, 2dc in foll dc, 1dc in next dc, 2dc in foll dc, 1dc in each of next 22dc, 2dc in foll dc, 1dc in last dc, join with a ss in first dc. 54 sts.

2nd round: 1ch, 2dc in first st, 1dc in each of next 24dc, 2dc in foll dc, 1dc in next dc, 2dc in foll dc, 1dc in each of next 24dc, 2dc in foll dc, 1dc in last dc, join with a ss in first dc. 58 sts.

3rd round: 1ch, 1dc in each of first 25dc, 2dc in each of foll 2dc, 1dc in each of next 27dc, 2dc in each of foll 2dc, 1dc in each of last 2dc, join with a ss in first dc. 62 sts.

4th round: 1ch, 1dc in each of first 25dc, 2dc in each of foll 2dc, 1dc in each of next 29dc, 2dc in each of foll 2dc, 1dc in each of last 4dc, join with a ss in first dc. 66 sts.

5th round: 1ch, 1dc in each of first 26dc, 2dc in foll dc, 1dc in each of next 32dc, 2dc in foll dc, 1dc in each of last 6dc, join with a ss in 1ch. 68 sts.

6th round: 1ch, 1dc in each of first 26dc, 2dc in each of next 2dc, 1dc in each of foll 32dc, 2dc in each of next 2dc, 1dc in each of last 6dc, join with a ss in first dc. 72 sts.

7th round: 1ch, 1dc in each of first 27dc, 2dc in each of foll 3dc, 1dc in each of next 33dc, 2dc in each of foll 3dc, 1dc in each of last 6dc, join with a ss in first dc. 78 sts.

Sides:

1st round: 1ch (does not count as a st), miss first dc, working in back loops only, 1dc in each dc to end, 1dc in ss, join with a ss in 1ch. 78 sts.

2nd round: 1ch, miss first dc, 1dc in each dc to end, 1dc in ss, join with a ss in 1ch.

3rd–5th rounds: As 2nd.

6th round: 1ch, miss first dc, 1dc in each of next 28dc, 2dc in foll dc, 1dc in each of next 38dc, 2dc in foll dc, 1dc in each of last 9dc, 1dc in ss, join with a ss in 1ch. 80 sts.

7th and 8th rounds: As 2nd.

9th round: 1ch, miss first dc, 1dc in each of next 26dc, 2dc in foll dc, 1dc in each of next 39dc, 2dc in foll dc, 1dc in each of last 12dc, 1dc in ss, join with a ss in 1ch. 82 sts.

10th and 11th rounds: As 2nd.

12th round: 1ch, miss first dc, 1dc in

each of next 24dc, 2dc in foll dc, 1dc in each of next 40dc, 2dc in foll dc, 1dc in each of last 15dc, 1dc in ss, join with a ss in 1ch. 84 sts.

13th and 14th rounds: As 2nd.

15th round: 1ch, miss first dc, 1dc in each of next 22dc, 2dc in foll dc, 1dc in each of next 41dc, 2dc in foll dc, 1dc in each of last 18dc, 1dc in ss, join with a ss in 1ch. 86 sts.

16th and 17th rounds: As 2nd.

18th round: 1ch, miss first dc, 1dc in each of next 20dc, 2dc in foll dc, 1dc in each of next 42dc, 2dc in foll dc, 1dc in each of last 21dc, 1dc in ss, join with a ss in 1ch. 88 sts. Working 2 rounds straight in dc after each inc round, cont as foll:

21st round: 1ch, miss first dc, 1dc in each of next 18dc, 2dc in foll dc, 1dc in each of next 43dc, 2dc in foll dc, 1dc in each of last 24dc, 1dc in ss, join with a ss in 1ch. 90 sts.

24th round: 1ch, miss first dc, 1dc in each of next 16dc, 2dc in foll dc, 1dc in each of next 44 dc, 2dc in foll dc, 1dc in each of last 27dc, 1dc in ss, join with a ss in 1ch. 92 sts.

27th round: 1ch, miss first dc, 1dc in each of next 14dc, 2dc in foll dc, 1dc in each of next 45dc, 2dc in foll dc, 1dc in each of last 30dc, 1dc in ss, join with a ss in 1ch. 94 sts.

30th round: 1ch, miss first dc, 1dc in each of next 12dc, 2dc in foll dc, 1dc in each of next 46dc, 2dc in foll dc, 1dc in each of last 33dc, 1dc in ss, join with a ss in 1ch. 96 sts.

33rd round: 1ch, miss first dc, 1dc in each of next 10dc, 2dc in foll dc, 1dc in each of next 47dc, 2dc in next dc, 1dc in each of last 36dc, 1dc in ss, join with a ss in 1ch. 98 sts.

36th round: 1ch, miss first dc, 1dc in each of next 8dc, 2dc in foll dc, 1dc in each of next 48dc, 2dc in foll dc, 1dc in each of last 39dc, 1dc in ss, join with a ss in 1ch. 100 sts.

39th round: 1ch, miss first dc, 1dc in each of next 6dc, 2dc in foll dc, 1dc in each of next 49dc, 2dc in foll dc, 1dc in each of last 42dc, 1dc in ss, join with a ss in 1ch. 102 sts.

42nd round: 1ch, miss first dc, 1dc in each of next 4dc, 2dc in foll dc, 1dc in each of next 50dc, 2dc in foll dc, 1dc in each of last 45dc, 1dc in ss, join with a ss in 1ch. 104 sts.

45th round: 1ch, miss first dc, 1dc in each of next 2dc, 2dc in foll dc, 1dc in each of next 51dc, 2dc in foll dc, 1dc in each of last 48dc, 1dc in ss, join with a ss in 1ch. 106 sts.

48th round: 1ch, miss first dc, 2dc in next dc, 1dc in each of foll 52dc, 2dc in next dc, 1dc in each of last 51dc, 1dc in ss, join with a ss in 1ch. 108 sts.

49th and 50th rounds: As 2nd. Fasten off.

HANDLE: (make 2)
With 5.00mm (UK 6) hook make 7ch.

Foundation row: 1dc in 3rd ch from hook, 1dc in each ch to end, turn. 6 sts.

Next row: 1ch (counts as first dc), miss st at base of ch, 1dc in each dc to end, working last dc in turning ch, turn. Rep last row until strip measures 38cm (15in) from beg. Fasten off.

Making up

Cut 4 pieces of plastic tubing, each 32cm (11½in) long. Wrap sticky tape around each pair and then place, centrally, on WS of each crocheted handle with 3cm (1¼in) of fabric at each end. Fold each long side of fabric around the plastic tubing and neatly slip stitch edges together. Place one handle, centrally, on top edge of bag front with ends 12cm (4¾in) apart and pin in place. Flatten strips at ends of handle and sew securely in place on RS of top of bag. Repeat with other handle on bag back.

Index

B

bags
    beach duffle bag 40
    bead-trimmed beach bag 56
    gingham shopping bag 104
    striped beach bag 28
    summer tote bag 124
    supersize bag 8
bath mat, fish 92
beaded curtain 116
boat motif 38

C

cardigans
    bold striped cardigan 32
    textured boxy cardigan 12
coat, poncho 80
curtain, beaded 116
cushions
    round cushion 120
    seaside cushion 36
    square cushion 120
    zingy round cushion 48

D

doorstop, handbag 16

F

fish
    decoration 30
    motif 94

H

hats
    Stetson-style hat 76
    sun hat with floppy brim 44

J

jacket, waterfall 60

K

kite motif 38

L

lace towel edging 100
lighthouse motif 39

P

placemats , mini rag-rug 84
ponchos
    poncho coat 80
    striped beach poncho 108

R

rugs
    mini rag-rug placemats 84
    shades of orange rug 112

S

scarves
    work-of-art scarf 64
starfish motif 39
sweaters
    colour-block sweater 96
    loop-neck sweater 88
    nautical sweater 68

T

throw
    colour-block throw 72
    funky throw 24
top, mesh-pattern 20

W

wrap, cobweb 52

Acknowledgements

Managing Editor: Clare Churly
Editors: Lesley Malkin and Eleanor van Zandt
Senior Art Editor: Juliette Norsworthy
Designer: Janis Utton
Production Controller: Sarah Kramer